CONFIDENT KIDS

Guides for Growing a Healthy Family

I Always, Always Have Choices

LINDA KONDRACKI

Fleming H. Revell Company
Tarrytown, New York

To Dr. Dale (Ryan), my friend and colleague, whose
encouragement and support enabled me to make one of the
wisest choices of my life–to step out in faith and share the
Confident Kids program with churches across America

Scripture is quoted from the
International Children's Bible, New Century Version,
copyright © 1986 by Sweet Publishing, Fort Worth, Texas 76137.
Used by permission.

Art direction and series design by Joy Chu
Production layout by Ellen Flaster
Illustrations by Cat Bowman Smith
Initial caps and logo on Read-Along Pages by Rita Pocock

Library of Congress Cataloging-in-Publication Data
Kondracki, Linda.
I always, always have choices / Linda Kondracki.
p. cm. – (Confident kids; 1)
ISBN 0-8007-5440-9
1. Child rearing–United States.
2. Decision-making in children.
3. Child rearing–Religious aspects–Christianity
I. Title. II Series: Kondracki, Linda. Confident kids; 1. HQ769.K5653 1992
649'. 1-dc20   92-903
CIP

Copyright © 1992 by The Recovery Partnership
Published by the Fleming H. Revell Company
Tarrytown, New York 10591
Printed in the United States of America

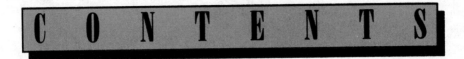

CONTENTS

If you would like more information about starting a Confident Kids Support Group program in your congregation or community, please write:

C O N F I D E N T   K I D S

℅ The Recovery Partnership
P.O. Box 11095
Whittier, CA 90603

About the "Guides for Growing a Healthy Family" Series

In a Nutshell...

The Family Guides are a collection of innovative books written especially for parents of elementary age children. More than a series of books about parenting, each book combines stories, discussion starters, and activities to create a practical hands-on resource parents can use to teach healthy living skills to the whole family.

Goals of The Series

THE FAMILY GUIDES ARE DESIGNED TO BE:

1. A "next step" resource for parents in recovery.

Each week in our country literally millions of people participate in recovery groups, support groups, inner child workshops, and/or individual, group, or family therapy. Through these resources they are confronting their destructive behavior patterns and doing the hard work of replacing them with new, healthier ways of living.

However, many parents in recovery are discovering that their individual recovery journey is not adequately preparing them to parent their children in healthy ways. Since our natural instinct is to parent in the same way we were parented, and since parents in recovery did not typically grow up in healthy homes with models of good parenting, they quite naturally feel at a loss when it comes to parenting their own children. Most recovery programs, however, do not go so far as to directly address how parents can translate what they are learning for themselves into the skills needed to parent emotionally healthy children.

The Family Guides can help parents in recovery take this "next step" by translating recovery issues into a form they can use with their children.

2. A tool any parent can use to teach healthy living skills to their children.

That's what good parenting is about–teaching children a set of skills to live healthy lives. But many parents today feel confused about what skills are needed to grow a healthy family and how to go about teaching those skills in the midst of the hectic, often fragmented family life so common in American homes today.

The Family Guides help with this task by identifying the key skills needed to build a healthy home and providing a practical, easy-to-use tool to enable your whole family to learn these important skills together.

3. A means to build family connectedness.

A common problem for families today is a loss of connectedness. Here again, hectic schedules, fragmented families, and a variety of other factors make it increasingly difficult for families to create the strong bonds needed to stay connected to one another.

The Family Guides help in this area by providing both the occasion and the agenda for spending meaningful time together. By using the unique resources of the Family Guides, your family will not only be learning new skills but also building bonds of connectedness that can be built only by spending quality time together.

A Unique Format That Combines Three Kinds of Resources

Each chapter in the Family Guides contains three sections, each of which is a distinct resource. It is the combination of these three resources that makes the Family Guides a unique and powerful tool. They are:

1. **Getting Ready (Parents' Pages)**
   Each chapter begins with a section for your own growth. Included in this section:

   ▶ Teaching pages, containing the main point of the chapter written at an adult level.
   ▶ Reflection questions to help you personalize the material.
   ▶ Key verses and short Bible studies to help you connect to God and His Word.

2. **Talking Together (Read-Along Pages)**

   The middle section "translates" the main point of the chapter into language your elementary age children will understand. Reading these pages together and talking about the questions will help you communicate valuable life skills information to your children. Included in this section:

   ▶ Teaching pages, written for elementary age children.
   ▶ A short activity.
   ▶ A story with discussion questions.
   ▶ A summary page clearly stating the main point of the chapter.

3. **Growing Together (Family Activities)**

   The final section is perhaps the most important one of all. Doing one or more of the suggested activities will not only reinforce the skill building but will also give you many occasions for bonding as a family. Included in this section are three kinds of family activities:

   ▶ **Building On God's Word.** Helps your family connect to God and His Word by memorizing key Bible verses and participating in short family Bible studies.
   ▶ **Conversation Starters.** These questions and activities will engage your family in significant conversations and sharing times.
   ▶ **Family Night Activities.** Choosing one or more of these activities will help your family enjoy a fun evening together and learn valuable skills at the same time. You will find instructions for a variety of things to do, including crafts, plays, cooking, family outings, and more.

How to Use
the Family Guides

FOLLOW THESE STEPS

Getting the maximum benefit from the Family Guides will take some planning and work on your part. Here is a suggested way to proceed:

1. **Choose a book that teaches a skill you would like to work on in your family.** Since there is no particular order to the series, you can start with any one of the books.

2. **Work through the "Getting Ready" sections yourself before getting the rest of the family involved.** Remember, you cannot teach a skill to your children that you do not have yourself. By working through the "Getting Ready" sections first, you will be better prepared to personalize the material to meet the unique needs of your family.

3. **Choose a period of time to work through the book with your family.** You will gain the most from each book in the series if you plan to work through it, covering one chapter each week. Mark off one evening a week for a family time on your calendar and be sure all family members understand the importance of being present for this time.

4. **Make thorough advance preparations.** Before bringing the family together each week, be sure you have prepared by:
   ▶ Reading all the pages in the "Talking Together" section and thinking through answers to the questions.
   ▶ Choosing the activity you would like to do and gathering all the necessary supplies.

5. **Gather your family and enjoy learning/playing together.** It is important for you to understand that, when used in real families, the activities and discussions do not always happen as perfectly as they sound in the book! In fact, you can be sure there will be many times when it seems your kids are not learning anything and you fear you are wasting your time. When those times come, remember two important points:

   ▸ Visible moments of growth will not happen every week.
   ▸ You are accomplishing a great deal by just being together.

   Perhaps the greatest benefit of using the Family Guides comes when you can relax and just enjoy being together as a family. Having realistic expectations will help you do that.

RULES FOR FAMILY INTERACTIVE TIMES

It must be kept in mind that the Family Guides are only a tool to help you create times of sharing and connectedness in your family. That can only happen, however, when the books are used in an atmosphere of openness and safety for all family members. You can make your family nights times of heart-to-heart sharing and fun for everyone by setting and consistently maintaining the following rules:

▸ **Family Rule #1: All family members actively participate in all family nights.** This lets everyone know they are an important part of the family. It also lets parents know they are expected to participate with their children, not sit on the sidelines and "let the kids do it."

▸ **Family Rule #2: All family members show respect for one another.** Mutual respect is the only way family members can feel safe enough to share openly. This rule means no put-downs, name-calling, hitting, or destructive behaviors of any kind are allowed during family sharing times!

▶ **Family Rule #3: Everyone speaks only for themselves.** In many families, one member often acts as the spokesperson for everyone else. This can be a child or a parent, but the result is the same: the other family members are not encouraged or permitted to express their own feelings or opinions. You will need to carefully monitor your sharing times to be sure all family members are encouraged to openly share what they are thinking and feeling.

▶ **Family Rule #4: No advice giving.** A continuation of rule #3, this rule is particularly important for parents whose communication style with their children tends to be one of lecturing or telling them what they should or should not do. Many parents see this as their primary role and do not realize that their well-intended advice often closes off communication with their children. Encourage all family members to speak only for themselves by eliminating "you should" or "if you would only" statements from your sharing times.

Of course, there will be those times when your children need guidance from you. If you sense a child needs help, try giving permission to ask for it. "Would you like some help in thinking that through?" or "I'd be glad to help if you need help with that" is much more affirming to a child than "you should" or "do it my way" messages. One word of caution: You must respect your child's right to say no to your offer of help. Hard as it may be to do, hold your advice until your child is ready to hear it.

▶ **Family Rule #5: It's okay to pass.** It is important to let everyone know they can be active participants and still have times when they do not feel ready to share their deepest thoughts and feelings. Sometimes the sharing may feel painful or threatening, and at those times family members need to have the freedom to pass. An environment is not safe if family members fear being pressured to talk about things they are not yet ready to share openly.

▶ **Family Rule #6: It's okay to laugh and have fun together.** In today's high-stress world, many families have lost the ability to simply enjoy being together. Give your family permission to use the activities as occasions to laugh, play, and make a mess together. You will find that much significant sharing and relationship building happens when family members are relaxed and enjoying one another's company!

There may be other family rules you would like to include for your family. Just remember that the purpose of each rule is to assure an environment that is safe, growth producing, and enjoyable for everyone!

TWO ADDITIONAL RULES FOR PARENTS
As parents, following two special rules will help you generate significant sharing in your family:

▶ **Parents' Rule #1:** Listen well! When asked what they most want from adults, children invariably report that they want to be listened to. Many parents unknowingly close off communication with their children by talking too much. Giving your children full attention and affirming what they are telling you will work wonders in building relationships with them.

▶ **Parents' Rule #2:** Share your own feelings with your kids. Modeling how to identify and talk about feelings is the best way to help your kids open up to you. Although you will need to use some discretion, letting your kids know that you feel a wide spectrum of feelings will teach them it is okay for them to feel, too.

An Important Note About Learning New Skills

Each of the Family Guides was written to help you and your family learn new skills for being a healthy family. The key point to remember as you start using the books is:

**Learning new skills takes time
and feels uncomfortable at first!**

Remember when you first learned to ride a bicycle or play a musical instrument or hit a baseball? It took time to learn the skills you needed to accomplish those tasks, and much of the time was spent in long hours of boring practice sessions. You probably also went through periods of discouragement thinking you would never improve or learn the skills you needed. But persistent work and practice eventually paid off and you gained the skills you desired.

Learning healthy life skills is like that. Being with your family in new, healthier ways will take time and commitment and a lot of patience to get through the times when you feel awkward and uncomfortable and as if things will never change. Remembering that you are learning new skills–just like learning to ride a bicycle or hit a baseball–can help you keep on.

STAGES OF SKILL DEVELOPMENT
Knowing what to expect can help you keep working during times when you may feel as if you are failing. The following acrostic will help you keep in mind what you can expect as you work on each of the skills in the Family Guides:

S = **Seeing the Need**
K = **Keeping On**
I = **Increasing Confidence**
L = **Letting Go**
L = **Living It**

S **Stage 1: Seeing the Need.** All change begins here. It is only when we are motivated by the need for change that we will go through the hard work of learning a new skill.

K **Stage 2: Keeping On.** This is the stage of greatest discouragement and the point at which most people give up. As you start practicing a new skill, you will naturally feel awkward and uncomfortable and will most likely want to revert to behavior patterns that are known and comfortable. At this point, you will need lots of encouragement and determination to keep going. Just remember:

I **Stage 3: Increasing Confidence.** Over time, you will begin to see changes, and the ability to use the new skill will take root. Learning to see and celebrate small steps of growth along the way will help build your confidence and keep you going.

L **Stage 4: Letting Go.** As you gain confidence and your skill level improves, more and more you will find yourself letting go of past behavior patterns and replacing them with the new, healthier ones.

L **Stage 5: Living It.** In this last stage, the new skill has become so integrated into your life that it becomes almost automatic. You find yourself using it easily and realize the hard work of the earlier stages has paid off!

There are no shortcuts to making healthy living skills a reality in your home. But you can do it, and the Guides for Growing a Healthy Family Series can help!

INTRODUCTION

"*I have* to do it. I just don't have *any choice!*" Those words have become "red light" words to me. Whether I say them to myself or hear someone else say them, it's as if a red light goes on in my head that tells me, "Stop! Remember, we *always* have choices! They may not be obvious at this moment, but we *do* have choices."

The choices we make from day to day set the direction our lives will take. One of the most important skills we need to live healthy lives is the ability to make wise choices, based on careful consideration of all our available options. In the chapters of this book, you and your family will learn a tool to help you make wise choices. We call it CHOOSE, and it is based on the following beliefs:

1. It is within my power to make wise choices in the circumstances of my life (I always have choices).
2. No one makes wise choices all the time. When I make an unwise choice, I can get back on course by acknowledging it, looking for a better choice to try, and asking for help if I need it.
3. Making wise choices is a skill that takes time and practice to learn. As a skill, I can learn it and I can teach it to my children.

CHOOSE:
Six Steps for Making Wise Choices

CHOOSE is an acrostic for the 6 steps for making wise choices. Those steps are:

C = **Claim the Problem.** Many times we make unwise choices because we try to avoid the problem at hand, or we don't think clearly about what our problem really is.

H = **How Many Choices Can I Find?** Remember, we always have choices. Sometimes we have to look hard to find them, but there are always choices available to us.

O = **Own God's Word.** Once we have found all our possible choices, we need a way to sort through them. God's Word contains a wealth of principles for healthy living. Eliminating options that disregard those principles can help us avoid lots of unwise choices!

O = **One Choice to Try!** By using several other criteria to evaluate our possible choices, we choose one we believe to be the wisest for this situation. Sometimes none of our options may seem that great, but at some point we must settle on one to try.

S = **See It Through.** There is a big difference between picking a plan of action and actually doing it. This step encourages us to follow through with our choice by taking risks and asking for help when we need it.

E = **Evaluate the Results.** When all is said and done, how do I feel about the choice I made? This is where we give ourselves (and our children) permission to say we made an unwise choice and that's okay, or we celebrate having made a choice we feel good about!

Remember, CHOOSE is a skill that takes time and practice to learn. Some of the steps may feel awkward and uncomfortable at first, but as you work through each step in the pages that follow, identifying options and choosing from among them will become an automatic response to the situations you face each day.

As You Begin Your Journey...

It is my prayer that CHOOSE will become a helpful tool for your family. In the weeks ahead, I hope you and your children will relax and have a good time together as you learn to CHOOSE!

CHAPTER

ONE

Choices, Choices, Everywhere!

GETTING READY

What's My Decision - Making Style?

I stood at the counter at McDonald's, staring at the menu, torn between ordering a Big Mac or a Quarter Pounder with cheese. Or maybe a Filet of Fish. And of course, fries, for sure. Or maybe a chocolate shake instead. After about fifteen minutes, and several shouts of "Come on, lady! We're hungry, too!" from the people behind me, I heard myself say to the clerk, "I'm sorry. I just can't seem to make one more decision today!" I was surprised by my own words. Until that moment, I hadn't realized I'd made enough choices in that day to make me feel so paralyzed! (I ordered the Big Mac, fries, *and* a chocolate shake! Bad choice. I couldn't eat it all.)

Every day we make hundreds of choices, most of the time without ever realizing we're doing it. We're just living life. But from the moment we open our eyes in the morning, we are making choices that will determine how the rest of our day will go:

▶ Will I get up now or hit the snooze alarm one more time (and probably be late for work)?

▶ Will I take time for breakfast or eat a donut at coffee break (and feel guilty about the calories the rest of the day)?

▶ Will I stop the kids from fighting now or wait until they draw blood?

▶ Will I mow the lawn tonight or wait until tomorrow night (I'm *sure* I won't feel this tired tomorrow)?

As long as the choices we make are small, we don't think much about them. They just sort of happen from day to day. It's when the emotional investment is high that our attitudes about making choices begin to surface. Notice the difference in feeling level between this list and the one above:

▶ A person who is on the same salary level as me just received a nice raise, and I didn't. How will I talk to my boss about it?
▶ A friend just called to tell me my child beat up his child at school today. How will I deal with my child?
▶ My husband lost his job because of his drinking. What will I do now?

We all have our own way of dealing with choices like these. We can call this our decision-making style. Like many of our approaches to life, our ability (or inability) to make choices was formed early in life. What was going on in our families in those days, what we saw in the way our parents made decisions, and how they treated us in our decision making has everything to do with how we make choices today. For instance, can you see characteristics of yourself or your family of origin in any of these decision-making styles?

▶ **Victim.** I have no choices of my own; I am at the mercy of my circumstances and controlled by the people in my life.
▶ **Impulsive.** I impulsively do the first thing I think of to do; I never think about the consequences of my choices.
▶ **Prophetic.** I know that I will always choose the wrong thing–always. And so I do.

‣ **Avoidance.** I am so scared of making wrong choices that I put off making a decision until the last minute. By then, I'm panicky or it's too late and I don't have a choice left to make.

‣ **Vengeful.** I will choose whatever will hurt others who have hurt me. I don't think about the consequences for myself, only how it will affect "the other."

‣ **Logical.** I make carefully thought-out choices that make perfect sense. I never make important decisions based on instinct or feelings.

Perhaps you can identify a different style for yourself; this is certainly not an exhaustive list. The point is that how we handle making choices is one of the most important skills we need to live a healthy life. If you are in recovery, you know that all too well.

In recovery, we learn to face the destructive cycles of our lives, one of which is a long history of making poor choices. But we *can* break those cycles by letting go of our unhealthy styles of decision making and learning new, healthy skills for making wise choices.

This book will help you do that by teaching you a six-step process we call CHOOSE. As you learn the steps of CHOOSE and teach them to your children, you will be developing a decision-making style that looks like this:

I make careful choices, following a process that blends thoughtfulness and instinct. I feel confident in my ability to make wise choices most of the time, but I know it's not the end of the world if I make a wrong choice.

For Reflection

1. How would you describe your decision-making style?

   _____

   _____

   _____

   _____

2. What was the predominant decision-making style in your family of origin?

   _____

   _____

   _____

   _____

3. When you were growing up, what happened when you made a poor choice?

   ☐ **a**   You got a lecture: "How many times have I told you...!"

   ☐ **b**   You were put on a guilt trip: "How could you do this to us?" or "I'm so disappointed in you."

   ☐ **c**   You were shamed: "You good-for-nothing! Can't you ever do anything right?" or "You keep that up and no one will ever have anything to do with you!"

   ☐ **d**   You were affirmed and encouraged to try another approach next time.

   ☐ **e**   Other:

   _____

   _____

   _____

4. What insights do you see between #1 (your present decision-making style) and #2 and 3 (life in your family of origin)?

   _____

   _____

   _____

   _____

Building On God's Word

**If any of you needs wisdom, you should ask God for it,
God is generous. He enjoys giving to all people, so God
will give you wisdom.** *James 1:5*

We are capable of making wise choices, but it's not always easy.
There is hope and good news in the fact that we are not alone.
Keep this special promise from God's Word close by throughout
your journey of learning to CHOOSE.

Choices, Choices, Everywhere!

Did you know that every day we make hundreds of choices? Some choices are so easy we don't have to think much about them, like choosing to brush our teeth before we go to bed or which cereal to have for breakfast. Others are fun and we might enjoy taking extra time to make them, like choosing an ice cream flavor for a double-dip cone or which present to open first on Christmas morning. Some of our choices are harder to make because they feel scary or confusing, like choosing whether or not to tell your mom that you were the one, not your little brother, who broke the lamp or deciding whether or not to watch a scary movie with your friends, even though you'd really rather not.

Making choices isn't always easy. Sometimes we make choices that make us happy and we feel really good about having made them. We'll call these **wise** choices. Sometimes we make choices that get us into trouble and we end up wishing we had not made them. We'll call these **unwise** choices. The thing about choices is that *everyone* makes some wise choices and some unwise choices; that's just the way it is. However, some people are better at making wise choices *most* of the time, while others seem to make *unwise* choices most of the time. Of course, the more wise choices we make, the better our lives will be. That's what this book is all about: helping you learn a way to make *wise* choices *most* of the time!

The first thing we must know to choose wisely is the difference between wise and unwise choices. Here are some ways to tell:

Wise choices...

▶ help me grow

▶ help me feel closer to friends and family

▶ feel good inside

Unwise choices...

▶ hurt me or someone else

▶ make me feel distant from friends and family

▶ feel bad inside

You can probably think of some other ways to tell the difference between wise and unwise choices. If you can, add them to the list above. Then use the list to decide whether each of the choices described below was a wise or unwise choice. If you think it was wise, draw a line from that statement to the word **wise**. If it was unwise, connect it to the word **unwise**.

WISE   **UNWISE**

1. Julia is very upset about her parents' divorce, but she chooses not to tell anyone about it.

WISE   **UNWISE**

2. Ryan feels stupid because he is having lots of trouble understanding his math

problems, so he chooses to ask his teacher for extra help.

3. Write your own example of a wise choice:

WISE _____ **UNWISE**
_____
_____
_____
_____

4. Write your own example of an unwise

WISE choice: _____ **UNWISE**
_____
_____
_____
_____

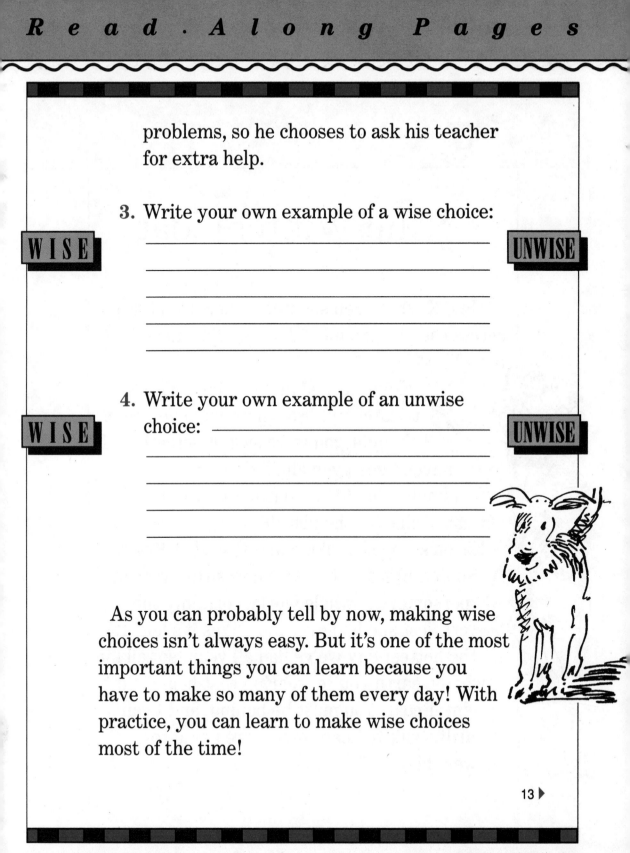

As you can probably tell by now, making wise choices isn't always easy. But it's one of the most important things you can learn because you have to make so many of them every day! With practice, you can learn to make wise choices most of the time!

13 ▶

(answers: #1 - unwise, #2 - wise)

The Winter Coat

"Hey, Kev!" Karen shouted to her friend from across the playground. "Wait up. I'll walk you home!"

Kevin turned and waited for Karen to catch up. "So where have you been? I thought you were sick or somethin'. I haven't seen you all day! You know what? It sure is hot today! I'm sweatin' all over the place!"

Karen stopped walking and stared at Kevin. Sometimes she thought he was the craziest person in the whole world, certainly the craziest she had ever met. "Yes it's hot! It's the hottest day we've had all year...so tell me why on earth you're wearing that heavy old winter coat. You must be boiling, and I can hardly wait to hear how you're going to answer this one!"

"It's simple, really. This morning, when I got ready for school, I decided to wear the first thing I pulled out of my closet. So, I closed my eyes and reached in and...presto! I had this in my hand when I pulled it out! So I decided to wear it."

"What a dumb choice! It must be 90 degrees outside today!"

"Not so dumb! The air-conditioning was turned up really high today. Didn't you think it was cold in school? Everyone else did!"

"Well, I was cold. I guess you made a good choice after all!"

"Not really. Billy saw me at lunch and made fun of me in front of all the other kids."

"Not again! Someone should do something about that bully! So, I bet you wish you hadn't worn that coat."

"No, I'm glad I did. This time I decided to stand up to Billy. I actually slugged him in the nose!"

"Good for you! Great choice!"

"Nuh-uh...bad choice! Miss Blakely saw me and I got in trouble. She said I had to choose between staying after school and going to the principal's office."

"That's awful! Tough choice...."

"No, it was easy. I choose to stay after school so Billy couldn't get me back on the way home!"

"Hey, good thinking! I probably wouldn't have thought of that."

"Of course, I forgot that Billy lives next door to me. He's going to be waiting for me when I get home."

"Oh, Kev, what are you going to do? He'll pound on you for sure! Maybe we should take the long way home and you can sneak in the back door or something."

"Nope. I choose to go home this way. Don't forget, Billy always hits me in the stomach, and I'm wearing this heavy winter coat.... Hey, Karen, what's wrong with you? You look mad or somethin'!"

"Kevin, you're crazy! Even I'm having trouble following you this time! First I say 'That's bad,' and you say, 'No, that's good.' Then I say, 'Oh that's good,' and you say, 'No that's bad.' This all started because you chose to wear that dumb coat to school this morning! Come on, Kev, which is it–good or bad–that you decided to wear a winter coat to school today?"

Kevin stared thoughtfully up into the sky for a few minutes. "Well," he said slowly. "I guess I'd have to say..."

What do you think?

▶ How will Kevin answer Karen's question?

▶ Make a list of all the different choices Kevin made. Decide which ones were wise choices and which ones were unwise choices.

▶ Can you think of a time you made a choice like Kevin's?

Remember...

It's not always easy, but...

You can make wise choices!

You can also count on God to help. Here's a promise from the Bible for you to remember as you learn to CHOOSE:

If any of you needs wisdom, you should ask God for it. God is generous. He enjoys giving to all people, so God will give you wisdom.   *James 1:5*

Growing Together

BUILDING ON GOD'S WORD

Memorize James 1:5. Make it a game around the dinner table (or sitting in the living room) by having one person in the family say the first word of the verse, the next person say the second word, and so on around the table until the whole verse is said correctly. If someone misses, the next person must start over with the first word.

CONVERSATION STARTERS

Play "Choices I Made Today." You can play this game with the whole family gathered around the dinner table, or individually with a child as you tuck him or her into bed. Begin by asking each person present to tell about one choice he or she made today and whether it was a wise or an unwise choice. When a family member shares about an unwise choice, think together about other choices that could have been made. (Caution: Be sure this does *not* become an occasion for you to "preach" or "lecture" to one another.) Play as many rounds as time allows. Examples to get you started:

- ▶ I chose to wear my green skirt to school today. I was comfortable all day; it was a wise choice.
- ▶ I chose to drink a cup of coffee with my pie at the restaurant tonight. It was an unwise choice; I feel wide awake and it's past my bedtime! (Parents play, too!)

▶ Darrel started to tease me in front of the other kids. I was really mad, but this time I chose to walk away. I think it was wise, but I still feel bad inside.

FAMILY NIGHT ACTIVITIES

1. **Learn From Watching TV Together.** Provide an occasion to practice distinguishing between wise and unwise choices by watching a TV program together. Families with younger children can choose a favorite family situation comedy. Families with older children can try a dramatic series or, if you are feeling particularly talkative, an afternoon soap opera. If possible, videotape the show first so you will have the flexibility to replay scenes, if desired. As you watch, make a game of identifying choices that are being made by the characters in the show. Designate one person as the secretary to write these down. After the show, serve your family's favorite dessert and talk about what you just saw:

▶ Review all the choices that were made during the show. What happened as a result of each one?
▶ Which choices were wise? Which were unwise? Why?
▶ In the case of each unwise choice, what other choices could that person have made?
▶ If you had been each character, what choice would you have made in that situation?

Growing Together

2. Take a "Penny Ride." As a fun way to illustrate the importance of good decision making, take a "Penny Ride." Pile the whole family into the car and tell them that you will be going somewhere special, but you're having trouble choosing just where that will be. Take out a penny and begin your journey by flipping it. If it comes up heads, pull out onto the street and turn right; if it is tails, turn left. Drive for about 30 seconds and at the next intersection, flip the coin again, turning right or left as the coin dictates. Proceed on your trip in this manner for as long as it holds the interest of your family. You can add interest by letting family members take turns deciding how long you will drive before turning and then "choosing" where you will go by flipping the penny.

21 ▶

C=Claim the Problem!

GETTING READY

What's the Real Problem Here?

I t was four o'clock in the morning as I lay on my bed listening to my college roommate pour out the painful details of something that had happened during the day. It was not an unusual scene. She was very open with her feelings and "spilled over" whenever anything of significance happened. I, on the other hand, was uncomfortable with sharing my own feelings with anyone but considered myself a good listener if others wanted to "dump" theirs on me. And, for some reason I never quite understood, those dumping times often occurred in the wee hours of the morning.

According to the usual pattern, it was about time for her to be winding down and I was already beginning to drift off to sleep. But this night we did not follow the "usual pattern." Instead, I was jolted awake by something she said, something I'd never heard anyone say to me before.

"Linda," she said in an angry tone that got my attention, "I swear that talking to you is like talking to a brick wall! And what's more," she added the final zinger with just the right flair, "everyone else around here thinks so, too!" At that, *she* drifted off to sleep, and *I* spent the rest of the night staring into the darkness.

So many thoughts went through my mind that night. I tried every way I could think of to deny what I had just heard. "She's just upset; she didn't really mean it," and, "so I'm a little reserved; so what?" and, "I'm sure everything will look different in the morning." But things didn't look different in the morning, and for the next three days I struggled with a problem I didn't want to face—a problem with my emotional life. Scary stuff. Of course, I'd never been presented with an occasion to think much about that area of my life. Until now.

I found myself with a choice to make: Would I choose to accept this information and do something about it, or would I choose to dismiss it as an isolated comment made in the heat of an emotional moment? I found myself more scared than at any other time in my life. I was scared to admit my roommate's accusation (or should I call it "feedback"?) was true, and even more scared to think of what would come next if I did! I wasn't sure I could face all of that. It would be so much easier to simply forget about it and go on with my life.

Many of life's unwise choices are made because we are afraid to look at what's real. There may be many reasons for our fear. We might be afraid that the truth will be too overwhelming. (What if everyone *does* think I'm like a brick wall?) We might be afraid of failure. (Maybe I can't ever be any different than I am!) Certainly, we fear being shamed. (I can never go out in public again; *everyone* thinks I'm a brick wall and they don't want to have anything to do with me!)

Reactions such as these to the problems life brings our way are natural; *everyone* fears they will be overwhelmed by the truth or unable to handle it "right" or shamed by the belief they have failed, and so on. Feeling those fears is normal and healthy. *Making choices* based on our fears is *not* healthy. When we do, we usually end up in a destructive cycle of making unwise choices that looks something like this:

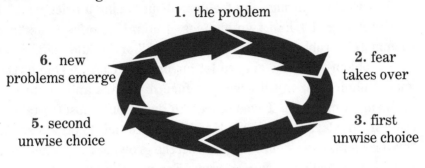

1. the problem
6. new problems emerge
2. fear takes over
5. second unwise choice
3. first unwise choice
4. guilt/shame

1. A problem surfaces about which I feel stressed and/or fearful.
2. Although there are some real fears involved, they become so strong I spend more time thinking about them than I do the real problem. (What will people think if they know I just got fired from my job? Who will hire me when they find out?)
3. Out of my fear, I make a choice that is not healthy or helpful (lie, have an affair, scream at the kids, get drunk, isolate myself, etc.).
4. I realize I made an unwise choice, and I feel guilt or shame.
5. Rather than accepting the fact that I made an unwise choice and going back to the problem at hand, I make another unwise choice to try to cover myself (tell another lie, deny the affair, blame someone else, get drunk again, etc.).
6. This creates a whole new set of problems that also feels stressful and fearful, and the cycle begins all over again.

Getting out of this cycle of making unwise choices is not easy, but it is worth the work! The first step is to embrace our fears and work toward making a healthy choice based on what the problem really is. To put it another way,

C = Claim the Problem.

As I worked through my feelings about "being a brick wall," I finally realized I had two choices. I could dismiss it as "my roommate's problem—she's *too* emotional," or I could claim it as "*my* problem—I'm not able to let anyone get close." One of the wisest choices of my life was to face my fears and claim the problem as my own. I was scared to death but chose to take a risk. In the days that followed, as I began to talk to others about "my problem," I was encouraged with the growing confidence that what I was dealing with was real. For me, the cycle of making unwise choices was cracked in those days when I first learned that claiming the *real* problem, whatever it is, has far greater rewards than giving in to fear.

F o r   R e f l e c t i o n

1. In your family of origin, can you identify any problems that were *not* claimed? Think of things like family secrets, the way conflict was handled, relationships with relatives or neighbors, and so on. Make a list of as many as you can remember.

2. Create a chart of your ability to claim problems and deal with them in healthy ways by marking how far along you are on each of the continuums below:

Deep denial   Deal with what's real

├─────┼─────┼─────┼─────┼─────┼─────┤

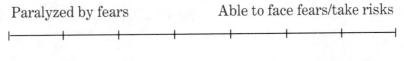

Paralyzed by fears

Able to face fears/take risks

├────┼────┼────┼────┼────┼────┼────┤

Never talk about
my problems

Have a network of
friends/helpers

├────┼────┼────┼────┼────┼────┼────┤

3. Do you see any relationship between #1 (family of origin) and
    #2 (current ability to face life's problems)?_____
    _____
    _____
    _____

4. What is your greatest decision-making situation right now?
    What fears are you feeling?
    What risks are involved in facing what's real?
    Whom can you trust to help?

Building On
God's Word

Read Luke 15:11-24. Jesus told this story about a young man
who got caught in a cycle of poor decision making. As you read
these verses, look for the following:

1. A cycle of unwise choices (verses 11-15)
2. An example of breaking the cycle by "claiming the problem"
    (verses 16-20)

3. The result of facing his fears and dealing with what was real (verses 19-24)

By telling this story, Jesus let us know that God understands about getting caught in unhealthy decision-making cycles. He also gave us the good news that the cycle can be broken, and just as the father in the story welcomed his son, we can count on God to receive us and stand next to us in our own journeys.

TALKING TOGETHER

C = *Claim the Problem!*

Which of these things are easy for you to do:

Ride a bicycle

Tie your shoes

Play the national anthem on the piano

Get all the way through Super Mario Brothers
   on Nintendo

Read the encyclopedia

Catch a ball

Bake a cake

Eat a hot fudge sundae

Make wise choices

29 ▶

Why are some things on this list easy for you, and others hard? Mostly it's because anything you do—like riding a bike or tying your shoes—is a lot easier once you've learned how to do it. Remember when you didn't know how to tie your shoes? It seemed hard and frustrating and took a lot of time to get it right. But then, once you learned what to do and had time to practice doing it, it was easy, and you probably can do it now without even thinking about what you're doing.

Making wise choices is like that. It's not something we just know how to do. Sometimes we may feel the way we did when we didn't know how to tie our shoes—like it's too hard, and we'll never get it right. But it's easier when we know how, and with practice, we can get good at it without even thinking about what we're doing. This book is helping you learn how to make wise choices. There are six steps to follow. To help you remember them, each step begins with the first letter of the word CHOOSE. In this chapter, we'll talk about step 1:

C = Claim the Problem

There are two important words to remember in step 1. They are as follows:

1. Claim the *Problem* tells us that life is full of problems we must solve by deciding what to do about them. Some problems are easy to solve and others are hard. But problems are just a part of life. Everyone has them. We can face any problem life brings our way by using the six steps for making wise choices (CHOOSE) to figure out what to do about them.

2. *Claim* the problem tells us that the place to start is to face up to whatever problems come our way. Sometimes we don't want to face something, and so we pretend it is not there. We hope that if we ignore it, it will just go away. Unfortunately, problems don't "just go away" by themselves. Ignoring our problems only makes them worse. Facing up to them (claiming) is the first step to solving them.

Sounds easy, doesn't it? But some problems are harder to claim than others, and we might

31 ▶

feel afraid to face them. There are lots of things we can be afraid of. Like getting in trouble with Mom or Dad or your teacher at school. Or losing a friend. Or looking dumb in front of the other kids. You can probably think of other things that make you afraid to face a problem. Whatever you fear, here's an important point to remember:

> **It's okay to be afraid when we have to claim a difficult problem; it's *not* okay to make an unwise choice just because we're scared.**

For example, it's okay to be scared to tell Mom or Dad that you were the one who broke the window — who wouldn't be scared to do that? But choosing to lie about it or blame someone else is *not* claiming your problem. Those are unwise choices that will most likely make things harder.

Here's a list of problems. Take a moment to think about each one. Draw a check ✔ next to the ones that would be easy for you to claim, and an ✘ next to the ones that would be hard:

▶ You got 3 *D*s on your report card. ☐

▶ You left the gate open and your dog ran away. ☐

▶ Your teacher accused you of something you didn't do. ☐

▶ You got ten dollars for your birthday and Mom wants to know what you're going to do with it. ☐

▶ They're all out of your favorite flavor at the ice cream parlor. ☐

▶ You hurt your best friend's feelings and now she (he) won't talk to you. ☐

Write a problem that is easy for you to claim: _____

_____

_____

_____

Write a problem that is hard for you to claim: _____

_____

_____

_____

So, what can you do when you have a problem to face up to and you're scared? You can remember that claiming your problem is always better than running away from it. And don't forget to ask for help if you need it!

Get Out Of My Face!

Jolene hurried away from the playground. She just didn't feel like talking to anyone right now. And maybe, if she walked very quickly, Georgie wouldn't see her before she got home.

"Hey, Jolene, where's the fire? Where ya going?"

This was the voice of her friend Josh, but she didn't even want to talk to him today. She heard running footsteps behind her.

"Hey, didn't you hear me? Slow up, will you?"

"Oh, hi, Josh," Jolene greeted her friend without slowing down or looking at him. She just stared ahead and kept walking—fast.

"Wasn't that a great lunch we had today? Everyone was havin' contests to see who could make designs in the Jell-O! Did you see what Jackson did to his whipped cream...hey, slow down, will ya?"

"I don't want to."

"What *is* the matter with you? You're actin' like—wait a minute! I'll bet I know!" Josh grabbed his friend by the arm and made her stop. "It's that bully guy, Georgie, isn't it? He's still bothering you, isn't he? Well, isn't he? Come on, Jo, talk to me!"

"So what if he is? It's none of your business, Josh, so just stay out of it!" Snapping her arm away, Jolene started walking again.

"Look, you can't let him bully you into giving him your lunch money every day! That's not right! You gotta do something to stand up for yourself!"

35 ▶

"Yeah, like what? He's about sixteen times bigger than me, and he lives in the next block. He said he'd sneak into our yard and clobber Alex if I didn't give him my money, not to mention what he'd do to me! I don't have any choice, okay?"

"That's not true and you know it! You always have choices. If you think about it, I'll bet you could come up with lots of ways to get rid of him!"

"No! He means it, Josh...and Alex is such a little dog! Knowing Georgie, he'd probably *sit* on him and smash him flat—and me, too! It's no big deal, okay? So I give him my lunch money, so what? Who cares, anyway?"

"I care! You're no fun anymore since Georgie started all this. Come on, Jo, I'll help you think about what to do. There's got to be—"

Jolene stopped abruptly, turned, and looked Josh right in the eyes. "Look, Josh, I told you I don't want any help! Now, would you please just *get out of my face!*" With that, she took off running, leaving Josh staring after her.

"Humph," he muttered. "Girls...who can figger 'em out?"

What do you think?

▶ What was Jolene's problem? Was she claiming it?

▶ Why do you think she wouldn't let Josh help her think about possible choices?

▶ Have you ever "not claimed" a problem like Jolene's? What happened?

Remember...

It's not always easy, but...

You can face your problems...even when it feels scary or hard!

And don't forget God's promise to help you know what to do. Can you say James 1:5 from memory? If not, look back to chapter 1 and read it again.

BUILDING ON GOD'S WORD

Keep a James 1:5 Journal. Review James 1:5, saying it together from memory, if you can. Then start a "James 1:5 Journal." Begin by decorating the cover of a notebook and writing the promise of James 1:5 in big letters on the first page. Talk together about one or two instances in the life of your family in which you are in need of God's wisdom. Record these in the notebook, and use them as prayer requests for a family prayer time. Add new requests as they come up from day to day. Be sure to write a few sentences in your journal every time you see an answer to your prayers for God's wisdom.

CONVERSATION STARTERS

Who Can Help Me "Claim My Problem"? Many of life's decision-making problems are difficult, and we need help to face them. Yet many of us have a difficult time asking for help when we need it. Give your children (and yourself!) lots of permission to ask for help when you need it. Use the following questions to guide your conversation:

▶ How do I know when I should ask for help with a problem I am facing? (Whenever I feel scared, confused, or I just want to talk about something.)

▶ Who can I ask for help? (Be sure every person in your family has a list of at least five sources of help. Your lists could include friends, relatives, counselors, teachers, coaches, etc.)

Take time to prepare a "Directory of Helpers" for each member of the family. Older children can make their own, including the names and phone numbers of those on their helpers list. Younger children will need help writing out names and phone numbers. For preschoolers who can't read at all, prepare a list with pictures of trusted adults they can turn to for help. Have all family members put their lists in a convenient place and use them whenever they need help.

FAMILY NIGHT ACTIVITIES

1. Make a "CHOOSE" Poster. Create a visual reminder of the CHOOSE process to post in a place where all family members can see it. Use a piece of poster board, and letter the heading across the top: **Let's Make Wise Choices!** Then write the letters of CHOOSE down the side. Fill in the first line, "Claim the Problem," using a different color marker. Keep the poster up and add each step as you learn it. Use it as a reminder whenever family members face decision-making situations.

LET'S MAKE WISE CHOICES!

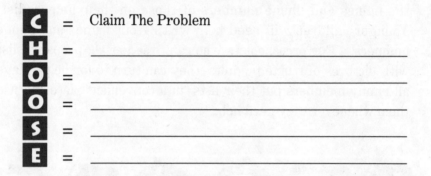

C = Claim The Problem

H = _____

O = _____

O = _____

S = _____

E = _____

2. Produce a TV Play About Making Choices. Combine your children's ability to learn through story and their natural love for the dramatic by producing a play of Jesus' story of the lost son. You will find a scripted version on the next page. Proceed as follows:

- ▶ Read the script together. Ask the kids to tell it back to you, so you are sure they understand the story line.
- ▶ Assign parts for the play. If your children cannot read, have a parent be the narrator, and let the other family members act out the scenes in pantomime style. Choose people to be the father and the son. Other family members can participate by being the townspeople and the pigs in the pigpen (they can do both).
- ▶ Practice the play, helping children think of ways to depict the action. For instance, the father can count out the money to the son; the son can turn his pockets inside out when the money is gone; and so on. Involve your kids in this by asking, "What can you do to show [whatever the scene calls for]?" You'll be surprised by their creativity. If you like, add some simple props and costumes.
- ▶ When you are ready, do the play all the way through. If there is some controversy over who gets to be the son, do the play again, giving someone else a chance to play the "lead."

FOR SMALL FAMILIES:

If you have only two or three people in your family, you could produce a radio show, using a cassette recorder to record the story. Use sound effects (coins clinking, crowd sounds, pig sounds, etc.) and music to add interest.

▶ 41

Growing Together

SCRIPT:
The Boy Who Claimed His Problem
From Jesus' Parable of
"The Lost Son," *Luke 15:11–24*

NARRATOR: Welcome to our show, "Stories Jesus Told." Tonight's episode features the story of a boy who got into trouble by making some unwise choices. Our story begins with a man who had two sons. One day the younger son knocked on his door and said,

SON: Father, I've been thinking. Why wait to give me my share of the inheritance you have set aside for us. Just think of all the things I could do with the money now. I'd like my share of our estate now.

NARRATOR: The father didn't think this was such a good idea, but he decided to give his son what he wanted. So, he counted out the money he had set aside for him. Not long after that, his son came to his father again and said,

SON: Father, I've been thinking. Now that I have some money, there is no reason I should stay here. After all, what is there for me here? I'm off to the city to make it big!

NARRATOR: Of course, the father didn't think this was such a good idea, either. But he decided to let his son make his own choice. So the son set off for the city, and there he had such great fun! He used his money to make new friends, throwing great parties with lots of food and drinks for everyone. He was a real

Growing Together

hit...until the day he discovered that all his money was gone, and he was in great need. Not knowing what else to do, he went knocking on the doors of his friends, looking for help.

SON: Hello in there...anybody home? Hellooo....

NARRATOR: From house to house he went, looking for help. But now that he had no money, he found he had no friends, either. Finally, he managed to find a job...feeding pigs on a local pig farm. After a few weeks of doing this, he became very sad and hungry and lonely. Then, one day, with his stomach growling, he started to think about—*choices!*

SON: I've made some pretty dumb choices, and look where they've gotten me! Here I am, feeding pigs and starving to death in this mud hole, while my father's *servants* have better lives than I do! But what can I do now? By now, I'm sure my father must think I'm a real jerk. I'll bet he doesn't even want me for his son anymore. Then again, maybe he would take me back as a servant! I could tell him, "Father, I am no longer worthy to be called your son; make me one of your hired hands. I'd rather work for you at home than here in this place!" I don't know what he'll say to that...he may throw me out on my ear...but I'm going to give it a try!

NARRATOR: So, the boy made his choice and started off toward home. While he was still a long way off, his father saw him and was filled with love for him. He ran to his long-lost son, threw his arms around him, and kissed him. The son cleared his throat...

▶ 43

SON: Ahem!

NARRATOR: ... and started his speech.

SON: Father, I have been so wrong! I'm not worthy to be called your son—

NARRATOR: But his father interrupted him, called for his servants, and said,

FATHER: Quick! Bring the best robe and put it on him. Put a ring on his finger and sandals on his feet. Bring the fatted calf and kill it. Let's celebrate! For this son of mine was lost to me, but now he's home! Let's have a party!

NARRATOR: And that's our story for tonight, about a boy who discovered that "claiming his problem" was far better than sitting in a mud hole with the pigs. Tune in next week for another episode of "Stories Jesus Told." Good night!

H=How Many Choices Can I Find?

GETTING READY

Choices! I *Always* Have Choices!

"That's not true," a mother of two young girls blurted out after I made the statement in a Confident Kids parents' group that we *always* have choices. She went on to say, "My ex-husband often shows up drunk when he comes to pick up the girls. I'm frightened to let them go with him, but the courts awarded him visitation rights, and by law I *must* let them go. *I don't have any choice!*"

One of life's most frightening circumstances is to feel trapped in a situation in which we feel we have no choices. "I just don't have any choice!" or, "There's nowhere for me to turn!" are words of powerlessness and hopelessness. Fortunately, in most of the situations we face, those words are *not* true. A fundamental truth to learn is this:

I always, always have choices!

Understanding this truth, and acting on it, is the way out of two common, unhealthy patterns of decision making:

1. **Victimization.** When we honestly believe we are trapped in a situation with no choices, we become victimized by that situation. Victims give away their power to make choices for themselves to other people in their lives:

- A wife feels she "must" stay with a violently abusive husband.
- A college student fulfills his parents' wishes by studying medicine when he would rather be studying teaching.
- Street kids get involved with gangs and then find they "can't" get out.
- An employee is "forced" into unethical business practices.
- Victims truly believe life has gone so far out of their control that there is nothing they can do but "make the most of" the situation at hand.

2. **Impulsivity.** Impulsive decision makers do the first or most obvious thing to do in a situation, without taking the time to think about all the options that are actually available to them. Like victims, they often feel trapped and powerless—not because they have *no* choices but because they choose too quickly. Many times, their impulsive choice makes the situation worse, resulting in feelings of failure and powerlessness. Their decision making sounds something like this:

"I just have to do what I have to do...that's all there is to it."
"I probably shouldn't have done that, but I didn't know what else to do!"
When presented with other choices in retrospect they reply, "Huh, I never thought about that!"

Both victims and impulsive decision makers can break their patterns by remembering:

I always, always have choices!

As we will see in the next chapter, sometimes our first choice is not available to us, and we can't have what we really want. Spouses file for divorce, people die, children do drugs, and there may be little or nothing we can do to change it. During those times, it is important to realize that, even though we may not be able to control the circumstances to get our first choice, that does *not* mean we are without choices. In any kind of decision-making situation, particularly when we feel trapped, we can do two things:

▶ *Stop and think* before deciding what to do next.
▶ *Make a list* of all the options available in this situation.

My personal rule is that I list as many options as I can possibly think of, *without passing judgment on any of them* (we'll talk more about choosing among available options in the next chapter). Then, when I have listed all I can think of, I look for two more. If I can't think of two more, I ask for help from trusted friends. When I'm through, I realize just how many choices are actually available to me, and the feeling of powerlessness is gone! As I shared this with the Confident Kids parents' group mentioned earlier, the group began to make a list of choices available to the mom who felt trapped by a law requiring her to put her children in an unsafe situation. Within a few minutes, we came up with a number of options, such as:

▶ Telling her ex-husband he can visit the girls only when he is sober.
▶ Giving the girls a choice of whether or not they want to go (she indicated that if the girls said no, the father would probably respect their choice).

▶ If all else failed, she could let the girls go and then immediately call the police and ask that her ex-husband be picked up for drunk driving.

All these ideas were new to this mom and helped her see that she did have choices in a seemingly hopeless situation. In later weeks, she kept us informed about which ones she tried and what happened as a result of each. Although the situation continued to be difficult to deal with, this mom felt a new freedom as she realized that she did indeed have choices available to her.

As parents, this is a particularly important skill to teach to our children. It gives them the tools they need to protect themselves from being victimized or acting impulsively, especially in those situations in which we are not available to guide or protect them. Growing up knowing that "I always, always have choices" is one of the most valuable gifts we can give our children!

F o r   R e f l e c t i o n

1. Presently, do you:
   ☐ **a** feel competent to find your own options?
   ☐ **b** look to someone (parent, spouse, friend, child) to tell you what to do (victim)?
   ☐ **c** limit your choices to the first few things that come to mind (impulsive)?
   ☐ **d** other?

2. Identify one area of decision making you are facing right now, and brainstorm a list of options open to you. List as many as you can possibly think of, but no fewer than five:

Option 1: _____

Option 2. _____

Option 3. _____

Option 4. _____

Option 5. _____

Option 6. _____

Option 7. _____

Option 8. _____

3. When your list of options is as long as you think you can make it, find two more. Ask for help from trusted friends if you need it.

_____

_____

Building On God's Word

Reread the parable of the lost son, Luke 15:11–24, and spend a few minutes reflecting on the point at which the son is sitting in the pigpen thinking about what to do:

▶ What might he have done/said from a victimization standpoint? ("I'm stuck here the rest of my life; I deserve this for being so bad.")
▶ What if he had been an impulsive decision maker? (He might have been thinking of stealing food or money, or he might simply have stayed "stuck in the mud," thinking that was all he could do.)

Is there an area of your life in which, like the son in Jesus'
story, you feel stuck in a "mud hole" and you can't get out? Bring
it to God right now, asking for His wisdom and help to discover
new options available to you.

TALKING · TOGETHER

=How Many Choices Can I Find?

Have you ever heard yourself saying these words?

"I *had* to do that! I didn't have any choice!"
"She made me do it!"
"I'm bored...there's nothin' to do."
"It wasn't my fault...he started it!"

Sometimes we find ourselves in situations in which we think we just don't have any choices.

At those times, it's important to remember that:

We always, always have choices!

It may not always seem so at first, but we do have choices. That's what step 2, "How many choices can I find?" is all about. It tells us two very important things:

1. There are always lots of choices for us.
2. We may have to look hard to find them.

Finding all our choices isn't always easy, especially during those times when we can't have our *first* choices. Take Gina, for example:

On Saturday morning, Gina's mom told her she had to clean her room—right now, and no excuses! Gina was just getting ready to go outside to ride her bike. But now she has to clean her room. She doesn't have any choice... right?

It's true that Gina doesn't have a choice about whether or not to clean her room. Mom was pretty clear about that. But she still has choices. In fact, what Gina chooses to do next is very important. Some of her choices are:

▶ She can mess around and try to avoid cleaning her room.

▶ She can try to sneak out of the house and ride her bike anyway.

▶ She can "Claim her problem" and get it done as quickly as possible so she can get on with what she really wants to do.

What other choices can you think of?

Can you see how the choice Gina makes next will either help her or make things harder? By taking the time to think about all the choices she can make, Gina can find the one that will be the most helpful to her. We'll talk more about that in the next chapter. For now, let's think more about how to go about doing step 2.

Finding all our choices takes practice. At first, it may be hard to think about all the choices we have. Most of us give up too soon, thinking we just don't have any choices, or we do the first thing that comes to mind. Making a list can help. Here's an example for you to try:

How many choices can you find for Joey? Write or draw them here:

Thinking about all our options is an important part of making wise choices. As you practice finding choices, it will get easier and easier to find them. Here's another story that can help you practice doing step 2.

Possible answers: 1. Get into a fight. 2. Walk away for a few minutes to cool down. 3. Ask for help from an adult. 4. Forget it and let him cheat. 5. Ask him to leave (or go home himself).

"I Didn't Have Any Choice!"

Maria's mom glanced at the clock as her daughter quietly slipped through the kitchen door. It wasn't like her to be home this early. She watched quietly as Maria opened the refrigerator door and stared at the milk and leftover mashed potatoes. "Hi, Mom," she said flatly, her eyes moving to the remains of last night's fried chicken and on to the jar of pickled beets.

"Well, well," Mom responded, as she finished the blouse she was ironing and hung it on a hanger. "Have a good day, did we?"

Maria kept staring into the refrigerator. "It was okay."

"Really? Is that why you're in here staring at

the leftovers instead of outside playing with Jana and Elsie?"

Maria slammed the refrigerator door and plopped down on a chair on the other side of the kitchen. "They're so dumb! I don't want to play with them ever again."

Mom nodded knowingly as she pulled Maria's favorite T-shirt, the one with the red-and-white stripes and yellow polka dots, from the ironing basket. "I've heard that before! So what happened this time?"

"You know that new girl who moved into the apartment in the next building? You know, the one with the kind of crooked leg?" she said as she took a glass from the cupboard and started back for the refrigerator.

"I think I've seen her walking to school a few times. She's usually by herself, isn't she?" Mom responded as she turned the T-shirt over on the ironing board.

Filling the glass with milk and taking the last apple from the drawer, Maria continued her story. "Yeah. She's kind of different in lots of ways. Anyway, today at recess Jana and Elsie and me were playing and this new girl was standing and watching us. She wasn't doing anything or saying anything, just kind of, well, staring at us. So Elsie started to giggle and pretty soon we were all laughing."

"And what did the new girl do?" Mom asked as she folded the red-and-white-striped T-shirt with the yellow polka dots and set it aside.

"She started to walk away. I think we hurt her feelings. But that's not all. When she walked away, Elsie started to make fun of that funny way she walks. Called her a lame duck and went, 'quack, quack, quack' loud enough for her to hear.

Jana thought that was funny, so she started doing it, too."

Mom set the iron up on end and sat down next to Maria. "And what did you do?"

"I started to do it, too," she answered quietly, without looking up from the stem she was twisting off her apple. Finally, she looked at her mom and blurted out, "But it wasn't my fault! They started it! What else could I do?"

"Maria, it sounds to me as if you didn't want to tease the new girl. Suppose you tell me what you could have done instead. And don't tell me 'nothin'! I know you can think of some other ways to handle a situation like that."

"Well, just what was I supposed to do? I could see the new girl was really hurt. But everyone at school thinks she's weird! So if I had tried to talk to her or stick up for her, they'd think I was weird and start making fun of me! I had to do it, Mom! I didn't have *any choice!*"

What do you think?
- ▶ What was Maria's problem? Did she claim it?
- ▶ What reasons did she give for choosing to do something she really didn't want to do?
- ▶ What other choices did Maria have, other than teasing the new girl? Make a list of as many as you can think of. Example: She could have walked away.

Remember...

No matter what situation you face,

You always, always have choices!

It may not seem so at first, but you can take time to think about what to do next. If you feel stuck, you can ask God to help! Remember God's special promise:

If any of you needs wisdom, you should ask God for it. God is generous. He enjoys giving to all people, so God will give you wisdom. *James 1:5*

BUILDING ON GOD'S WORD

Family Bible Study: "Stuck in the Mud." Read Jesus' story of the lost son (Luke 15:11–24) together, using your Bible or the script from chapter 2. Talk about the point at which the son finds himself in the pigpen:

1. What choices had the son made to get to this point?
2. What do you think the son was feeling as he started thinking about his father's house?
3. How many choices do you think the son had in that situation?

No doubt the son went through a time when he felt he didn't have any choice but to stay with the pigs. He probably felt alone, scared, and even ashamed that he had made some unwise choices. But by taking the time to think about all his choices, he discovered he didn't have to stay "stuck in the mud."

Making It Personal: Invite family members to share personal examples of times they felt "stuck in the mud" and didn't have any choices. Maybe something happened at school (work) or with friends or in your family, and you felt alone and scared. When you are through sharing, offer these words of encouragement: The next time you feel "stuck" in a situation, remember Jesus' story about the lost son, and follow his example—take time to think about all your choices! When you're done, you'll discover you're not "stuck" anymore!

Growing Together

A Family Prayer Huddle: Stand together in a circle with your arms around one another's shoulders and pray this prayer:

Dear God,

Thank You for teaching us that no matter what situation comes up in our lives, we always have choices! And thank You that You promised to give us the wisdom we need when we feel "stuck." [All family members shout "AMEN!" together.]

CONVERSATION STARTERS

Play "How Many Choices Can I Find?" Finding all our available choices is a skill we can learn. As with all skills, we improve when we practice! Use this game around the dinner table or when you have an extended time in the car. Start with a situation such as the ones listed below. Then take turns naming an option for that situation. When a family member cannot think of an option at his or her turn, he is eliminated from that round. Continue until all but one family member is left. Begin a second round with another situation.

You can find situations just about anywhere. TV or movies, storybooks, and the daily news are all good sources. Also, family members can make up situations or use situations from their own lives. Here are a few to get you started:

Growing Together

▶ Mom says we're going to visit Mr. and Mrs. Jones, and I don't want to go. (Possible choices: I can ask to stay home; I can ask to bring a friend; I can bring something to play with while they talk; I can throw a tantrum; etc.)

   ▶ I saw a friend steal something from the store. (I can tell the shopkeeper; I can talk to my friend about it; I can ignore it; I can steal something, too; etc.)

   ▶ I spilled my milk at the dinner table. (I can apologize; I can clean it up; I can blame someone else for bumping me; etc.)

FAMILY NIGHT ACTIVITIES

1. "Stuck in the Mud" Follow-up Activities. Begin your evening with the Family Bible Study (*see* "Building On God's Word" above) and end it with one of the following two options:

Make a Story Box. Young children will enjoy using a Story Box to retell Jesus' story of the lost son. You will need the following materials:

Growing Together

A shoe box
A 12" x 18" piece of felt or fabric for the story mat
5 roundheaded clothespins
5 small pieces of Play-Doh or clay
Scraps of fabric, felt, and yarn
A small container in which to make mud
Small plastic pigs, as from a farm set

Use the clothespins and fabric scraps to make people: the father, sons, and one or two townspeople (*see* illustration). Mix a small amount of dirt and water to make mud for the pigpen, and place the pigs in it. Kids can now use the figures to act out the story as many times as, and in whatever way, they wish. When they are through, clean out the "pigpen" and place all figures into the shoe box until next time.

Make a Real Mud Pie! Get the whole family into the kitchen and working together to make this pie. While it's baking, work on your CHOOSE poster (*see* below), and/or play a round or two of "How Many Choices Can I Find?" (*see* "Conversation Starters" above).

MUD PIE
(Old family recipe)

3 egg whites
3/4 cup sugar
1 teaspoon vanilla
3/4 cup chopped walnuts
3/4 cup chocolate wafer crumbs
whipped cream
chocolate sprinkles or shaved chocolate for garnish

Beat egg whites with a pinch of salt until soft peaks form. Add the sugar and beat until stiff peaks form. Add vanilla, walnuts, and wafer crumbs and fold together. Pour into greased pie pan and bake at 350 degrees for 30 minutes.

Cool and cover with whipped cream. Garnish with chocolate sprinkles or shaved chocolate. Place in the freezer and let set for about an hour. Store leftovers in the refrigerator or freezer.

2. **Add a phrase to your CHOOSE poster.** If you made a poster last week, add the phrase, "How Many Choices Can I Find?" to the next line. As an additional way to help family members remember the steps of CHOOSE, learn the motions that go with each step. For steps 1 and 2 they are:

Growing Together

"Claim the Problem." Cross your arms over your chest, as if embracing something.

"How Many Choices Can I Find?" Put your finger to the side of your head, as if thinking intently.

O=Own God's Word O=One Choice to Try

GETTING READY

Whatever Shall I Do?

Once we have claimed a problem and made a list of all the options available to us, we need to decide which one is the best in this situation. The next two steps of CHOOSE tell us to take the time to evaluate each option on our list and eliminate those that would lead to unwise choices. There are a number of guiding questions we can ask to help with this process:

1. **What Does the Bible Say?** Step 3, **O = Own God's Word**, is based on the belief that the Bible is a treasure chest full of principles for living healthy lives and a primary source for finding God's wisdom and guidance. Certainly, this is a belief that is shared by all Christians and needs no further explanation...or so I used to think. Until I met Betty.

   When Betty first asked to talk with me, I was apprehensive. What could I say to someone who did not seem to have one place of strength or joy in her life? After listening to her story for about an hour, it seemed to me that what she was lacking in her life was a nurturing, caring parent—the kind of parent only God could be for her. So I began to gently tell her of Someone who cared very deeply for her and could give her the strength to face the realities of her life. Then I took my Bible and began to read Psalm 139. As I read about a God who knows every detail of our lives and is always with us no matter where we go in the whole universe, I was sure this was just what Betty needed!

When I finished, Betty sat very quietly staring at the floor. I'll never forget her next words: "I *hate* that psalm," she said. Seeing the stunned expression on my face, she continued, "Don't you see? It just proves what I've been trying to tell you. No matter what I do or where I go, He's there, and He isn't *ever* going to let up on me! Sometimes I wish He'd just leave me alone!"

I learned a lot from Betty that day. I learned that not everyone experiences the Bible the same way I do. I learned that what to me is a treasure chest full of assurances of God's presence and tender care is for others a book about a God who sets up long lists of impossible rules and then "comes down hard" on us when we break them. And I learned that the promises of God's love that are so comforting to me are seen by others as having little application to the harsh reality of their lives. In the years since that day, I have come to appreciate that learning to embrace the Bible as a meaningful resource for life is a difficult and often painful part of the recovery journey.

The imagery of Proverbs 2:1–6 has been helpful to me in dealing with this issue. These verses have helped me picture the Bible as a treasure chest full of God's wisdom and guidance to face the decision-making points of our lives. However, it is a *buried* treasure. Before we can get to it, we have to search hard and dig deep through the distorted ways we have seen God and His Word in the past. Hard as that may be, it is worth the work! Knowing what the Bible says and following its principles *is* a treasure that helps us make wiser choices and live healthier lives.

2. Is There Something That Is Beyond My Control? Many times, the options we would most like to choose are unrealistic because other people or circumstances set boundaries that are beyond our control. For instance, suppose I am a "night person" and I'm having trouble getting to work on time because I do not function well in the morning hours. I may feel a realistic option for me is to change my work hours and come in at 10:00 A.M. instead of 8:00 A.M. However, if my boss doesn't see it that way, coming in at ten is an option that is beyond my control.

Understanding this point is crucial. Trying to change or fix things that are beyond our control is a terrible drain of energy and sets us up for failure. Knowing what is within our power to control allows us to face what is real and focus our energy on making the most of the situation.

3. Is It Destructive in Any Way? Our list of options may include choices that are potentially destructive to ourselves or to others. These options are never wise choices. For example, cutting ourselves off from friends and other support systems is harmful to ourselves. Getting revenge or "paying back" someone who has hurt us only makes things worse. We can find healthier ways to deal with our problems.

4. How Does It Feel Inside? Our internal feelings are an important source of guidance for making choices. This is another area that can be difficult for some. Many of us were taught *not* to trust our feelings to guide us. After all, feelings are unpredictable and too, well...too *emotional!* Although we cannot make our choices based on feelings alone, ignoring them is equally destructive. In fact, one of the functions of feelings is to help us get in touch with what is going on inside of us. Paying attention to uncomfortable feelings is part of making wise choices.

5. **What Do Trusted Friends Say?** Everyone needs help making choices. One of the skills of living is having a strong support network to turn to for help when we need it. Part of our network needs to be trusted advisors who can help us see clearly and make wise choices.

Here again, we must be careful. There is a difference between asking for help and looking for others to make our choices for us, or making choices to please others. This may be particularly hard when it comes to our relationship with our parents. I was thirty-one years old before I realized how much my parents' approval was affecting my decision making. As we work through our relationship with our parents, we must address this issue. If you seek your parents' guidance, is it because they are wise supportive friends or because you want to be sure you will *not* make another choice that will bring their disapproval?

As you can see by now, sorting through our options is not as easy as it sounds. Using guiding questions can help us keep in touch with our issues and bring us to the next step, **O = One Choice to Try.** This is the point at which we settle on one option as the one we will try in this situation. Sometimes the wisest option emerges very quickly, and other times we may not want to try *any* of our options. Just remember, O = One Choice to *Try*. Getting it right is not the point. Growing in our ability to make wise choices based on careful evaluation of all our options is our goal. We need not be paralyzed by fear that we are making a wrong choice or that we will fail. Rather, by taking the time to carefully think about each of our options, we can be confident that we have made the wisest choice we can—and move on.

For Reflection

1. What issues do you have that interfere with your ability to make wise choices:
   - ☐ Fear of failure
   - ☐ Need for approval from parents or others
   - ☐ Disconnection from the Bible as a Source of guidance
   - ☐ Lack of encouragement to make your own choices in your family of origin
   - ☐ _____
   - ☐ _____
   - ☐ _____

2. Word pictures can help us with our task of embracing the Bible. In the blank spaces below, list three word pictures describing what the Bible means to you. A few examples are listed to get you started.

   To me, the Bible is...
   - ▶ a portrait of all my failures
   - ▶ a treasure chest of God's love and wisdom
   - ▶ a Book written in another language—I don't understand it
   - ▶ a flashlight—helps me get through the times of darkness
   - ▶ _____
   - ▶ _____
   - ▶ _____

3. When you were growing up and found yourself wanting to do something with which you knew your parents would disagree, would you:

☐ absolutely *not* do it, even if you really wanted to and believed it was right.

☐ do it *because* they did not agree.

☐ do it, but be sure they did not find out about it.

☐ try to get them to see your point of view but make your own choice regardless of their feelings.

☐ feel it did not matter because there was no communication between you and your parents at all.

☐ agree to disagree, knowing they would be supportive of whatever you decided.

What implications do you see for the way you make choices today?

4. List below three counselors or trusted friends who can help you make *wise* choices:

a. _____

b. _____

c. _____

Building On God's Word

Making choices that are right for us is not always easy. God promises to give us His wisdom to help. Proverbs 2:1–6 compares

God's wisdom with a treasure of great value; it also implies it is a buried treasure:

> **Cry out for wisdom.... Search for it as you would for silver. Hunt for it like hidden treasure.... Only the Lord gives wisdom. Knowledge and understanding come from him.** *Proverbs 2:3–6*

List below the issues you may have to "dig through" in order to find the treasure of God's wisdom:

▶ Distorted images of God and/or the Bible
▶ The need for parental approval
▶ Bitterness toward others who have hurt you
▶ _____
▶ _____
▶ _____

Remember, finding buried treasure is worth the hard work it takes to get to it! Discovering and living by the principles of God's Word *will* help us make wise choices!

TALKING · TOGETHER

O =Own God's Word

O =One Choice to Try

Once we have claimed a problem and made a list of all the choices we have in that situation, we have to take the next step of deciding which one of our choices we will try. We can do that by stopping to ask ourselves some questions about each choice we have. We'll call these "guiding questions," and there are five of them:

1. **What Does the Bible Say?** Have you ever been on a treasure hunt? It can be exciting to go out searching for a chest full of wonderful treasures! When we think of treasure, we usually think of pirates and buried treasure—like in Pirates of the Caribbean at Disneyland! In fact, there are many people today who still believe there are real treasure chests that were buried by pirates and never found. Some people have actually quit their jobs and spent every penny they had to search for them!

   But treasures don't have to be jewels and gold coins and things worth a lot of money. A treasure can be anything that is valuable to us. Our treasures can include our most special toys, a ribbon or trophy won at a swim meet or state fair, or a photo album with pictures of the most special people and times in our lives. Many of our treasures wouldn't bring us very much money if we sold them, but they bring us something much more valuable: reminders of the best parts of our lives.

Did you know that the Bible is a treasure, too? It's a treasure because it gives us something very valuable: help in making wise choices in our lives. That's what step 3, **O = Own God's Word,** is all about. Learning what the Bible says and then "owning" it or doing the things it teaches us will help us make wise choices. Of course, learning all the things the Bible has to say takes a long time — like the whole rest of our lives! But you are not too young to start "owning" what the Bible says and using it to make wise choices. We'll see how it works a little later on.

2. **Is There Something That Is Beyond My Control?** That's a really important question, because many times the choice we would most like to make is *not* within our power to make happen. For instance, if your parents were getting a divorce, your first choice would probably be to have them get back together again. But that is a choice your parents must make and is completely beyond your control. As hard as it may be, you will need to cross it off your list of choices.

3. **Will It Hurt Me or Someone Else?** If your list of options includes ones that will hurt you, cross it off. For example, if someone is hurting you at home or anywhere else, keeping quiet about it is *not* a wise choice. In the same way, if one of your options is to hurt someone else, cross it off. Hitting someone, telling lies about others, and stealing their things are *not* wise choices. You can find other ways to deal with your problem.

4. **How Does It Feel Inside?** Listening to our feelings helps us make wise choices. If a choice feels wrong, cross it off your list. Be careful, though. Some choices may feel uncomfortable, but deep down inside we know they are wise—like choosing to tell the truth instead of covering up with a lie. But that's different from feeling uncomfortable because deep down inside we know it's wrong—like letting your friends talk you into shop-lifting, or letting someone touch you in ways you don't want to be touched. Our feelings give us valuable guidance. Learn to listen to what they are telling you!

5. Who Can Help Me Choose? Making wise choices is important enough that we may need to ask for help. Keep a list of people you can talk to whenever you feel confused or just don't know what to do.

These are all good questions to help us think about our choices and eliminate those that are unwise. That brings us to the next step, **O = One Choice to Try.** After we have looked carefully at all our choices, we will finally settle on the one we will actually use. Sometimes it can take a long time to make that choice, and sometimes we can do it very quickly. The important thing is to be sure we have considered all our options and feel we are making the wisest choice we can. Now let's practice using the guiding questions by helping Joy with her problem:

Joy loved
to play baseball

with her friends, and she was the best hitter in the neighborhood! Too good, in fact...this morning she hit a homer—right through Mr. Bartlett's window! They stopped the game and waited for him to come out and yell, but he never came. Joy looked over the fence and saw that his car was gone. "Lucky for us," all the kids said, "he'll never know who did it!" Then they all went home so no one would be there when Mr. Bartlett came home and found the broken window.

After lunch, Joy went to her room, confused about what she should do. She sure didn't want to get in trouble for breaking the window, but she was getting sick to her stomach, worrying about her parents' somehow finding out about what happened. Since Joy knew about CHOOSE, she got out a paper and pencil to make a list of all her choices. These are the ones she came up with:

▶ Just forget it, and hope no one finds out who did it.
▶ Lie and say she heard the window crash but she doesn't know who did it.

▶ Lie and say Mario broke it (which they would probably believe because Mario was always getting into trouble).

▶ Go to Mr. Bartlett and apologize and see what happens.

▶ Go to Mr. Bartlett and offer to rake his leaves to help pay for the window.

▶ Go to her parents and ask them to help.

▶ _____

_____

▶ O = One Choice to Try: _____

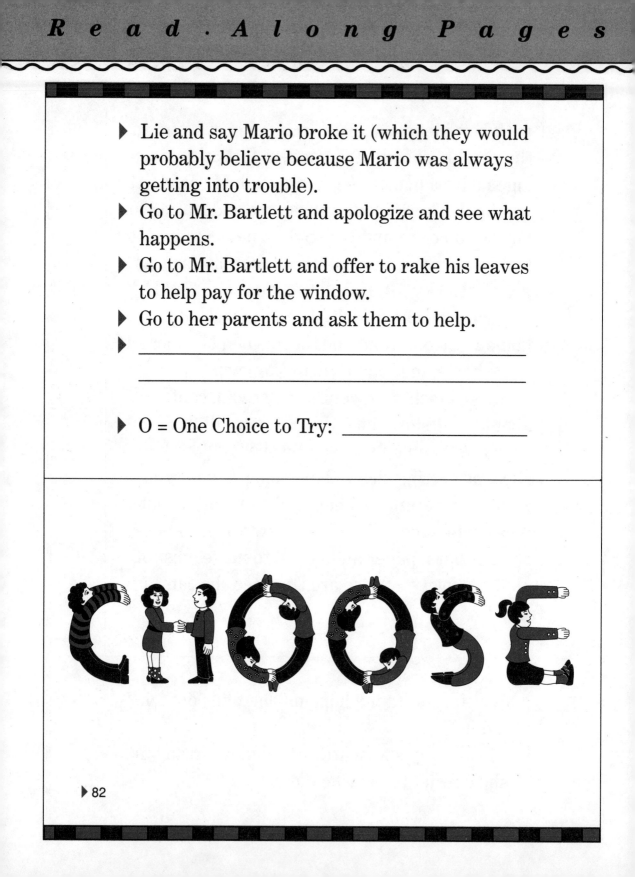

Can you think of any other choices to add to Joy's list? Write them on the blank lines. Now look back over the guiding questions and use them to help Joy think about each of her options. Cross out each one you think is unwise. Then decide which choice you think is wisest for Joy to try, and write it on the last line.

Get the idea? Here's another story to help you practice.

$\mathcal{O}$ops!

Robert and TJ walked out of the video arcade and started for home. "Gosh, TJ, that was *really* fun! Now aren't you glad you decided to go with me?"

"I guess so," TJ said, although his tone of voice said he wasn't so sure he was glad. Robert, however, didn't notice.

"The video arcade's my favorite place! I knew you'd like it, too! Your mom's crazy for not letting you go there. This little plan we came up with worked great, huh?"

"I guess so," TJ answered, still sounding unenthusiastic. "Oh, gosh, did you hear that?" he asked, grabbing his stomach.

"What? Are you okay?"

"Yeah, I'm just really hungry! Skipping lunch today so I'd have money for the arcade was sort of dumb."

"Nah! What's food compared with Star Crashers and Monster Stomp?" Finally realizing that his friend wasn't as excited as he thought he would be, Robert asked, "Hey, TJ, you did have fun, didn't you?"

"Yeah, sure...I guess. 'Cept I was so worried about what would happen if my mom ever found out that it sort of took some of the fun away. Not to mention how hungry I am!" He grabbed his stomach again as another rumble erupted from inside.

"Look," Robert said assuringly, "this is a great plan, you'll see! You tell your mom you're at my house studying for history or somethin' and we just sort of get sidetracked at the arcade on the way to my house. Would you stop worrying? She'll never know!" Looking right at TJ's stomach, he giggled, "And would you do something about that stomach of yours; you're gonna scare the neighbors!"

"Maybe I could get a snack or something at your house before I go home so my mom won't get suspicious."

"Okay, come on in," Robert responded as they started up the walk to his house.

As soon as they got through the door, Robert's mom was waiting for them. "There you two are! I've been waiting for you. I want to know where you've been and what you're up to!"

Robert and TJ looked at each other and said, "What do you mean?" at exactly the same moment. Robert added, "Mom, I told you we were going to the arcade after school, and that's where we were—honest!"

"Robert, you told me this morning that TJ's mom agreed to let him go to the arcade with you after school. TJ, your mom called here almost an hour ago and asked for you. She said *you* told her you were coming here after school to study for the history test tomorrow. She wanted to tell you to wait here and she would pick you up and take you out for pizza tonight as a treat for working so hard for that test! Now I think *you're* going to be the main course! And Robert," she turned and glared at her son, "you just might end up being dessert!"

The boys turned and looked at each other again, and said, "Oops!" at exactly the same moment.

What do you think?
▶ Make a list of all the choices TJ and Robert made in this story. Which ones were unwise?

▶ What other choices could they have made to help them get to the arcade? Think of as many as you can.

▶ Using the guiding questions you learned in this chapter, look at each option and eliminate the ones that are unwise.

Remember...

You can make wise choices by thinking carefully about what to do!

You can start by asking what the Bible says. Letting the Bible be our Guidebook is *always* a wise choice.

Growing Together

BUILDING ON GOD'S WORD

"The Bible Is..." Word Pictures. Help your children develop positive images of the Bible by finding word pictures to describe it. Begin by memorizing Psalm 119:105: "Your Word is like a lamp for my feet and a light for my way." Talk about its meaning:

▶ When are some times we need a "lamp for our feet"? (Any time we are stumbling around in the dark: camping, during a bad storm when there's a power failure, a nightlight to help us get to the bathroom, and so on.)

▶ How is God's Word like a light for us, especially when we need to make wise choices? (It helps us know what to do, especially when we feel confused or pressured to do something that feels wrong.)

Now think of other word pictures to describe what the Bible does for us. For instance, it's like a map to keep us headed in the right direction; it's a rule book like the one we have for Little League or that comes with Monopoly, etc. You might want to make a poster to visually depict all your word pictures!

CONVERSATION STARTERS

Read a Book Together. You can have many good discussions with your children by reading the book *Secrets of the Best Choice* by Lois Walfrid Johnson. This book is part of the "Let's Talk About It" series published by Navpress and is available through your local Christian bookstore. Each chapter contains a short story in

Growing Together

which a child must make a difficult choice. The questions and related Bible passages at the end of each story will help you practice identifying options and applying biblical principles to real-life situations.

FAMILY NIGHT ACTIVITIES

1. **Have a Treasure Party.** Combine learning about making wise choices with an enjoyable family evening or outing. Choose one of the following options:

Make a Treasure Box. You will need a variety of items for family members to create their own treasure chests:

Growing Together

Sturdy boxes with lids, like cigar or shoe boxes
Gold and/or silver wrapping paper
Gold and/or silver spray paint
Various sizes and shapes of macaroni, spray painted gold or silver
Old costume jewelry
White glue (you might want to also have a hot-glue gun available)

Keep the following items hidden until the end of your activity time:

▶ An assortment of small trinkets such as pencils, balloons, gold-foil-covered chocolate coins, gum, and so on.
▶ Small Bibles (with Psalms and Proverbs) or scrolls of Proverbs 2:1–6
▶ Copies of the guiding questions presented in this chapter

Cover the boxes with wrapping paper, or spray them with the gold or silver paint. Then let each family member make his or her own unique treasure box by gluing the macaroni and "gems" from the costume jewelry onto the boxes. Although the white glue should hold, parents may want to be prepared to fasten some things with a hot-glue gun.

When the boxes are complete, give them time to dry while you talk about the following:

▶ What kinds of things do we put into a treasure box? (Things that have great value; they cost a lot of money, or they have great meaning to us.)
▶ What would you like to place in your treasure box? (Send

Growing Together

family members on a "treasure hunt" to gather several small items they would like to keep in their boxes.)

As family members place their "treasures" into their boxes, ask them to tell why they chose the items they did. What special significance does each one have that qualifies it as a "treasure"? Then give each family member a Bible or scroll of Proverbs 2:1–6 to put into his or her box. As they do, remind them that God's Word is a treasure of guidelines to help us make wise choices and that learning what it says, and following these guidelines, is one of the wisest things we can do! Similarly, give out the copies of the guiding questions, reminding everyone of the value of thinking through all our options before choosing one to try.

End your time by bringing out the trinkets and letting family members add some new "treasures" to their boxes.

Go On a Treasure Hunt. Enjoy an outing to look for "buried treasure." This event will take some secret advance planning on the part of the parents, but it is well worth the effort!

First, prepare your treasure chest by gathering together a number of objects that are "treasures" to your family, such as a photo album or scrapbook of past special family events, birth certificates, special heirlooms, etc. Place these items in a large box or chest of some kind, *placing a family Bible and a nicely printed copy of the guiding questions learned in this chapter in with them.* If you like, include a few new "treasures," such as gold foil chocolate coins or little gifts your children will enjoy. Seal the box and decorate it to look like a treasure chest.

Next, choose a place to "bury" it. Depending on where you live, you could bury it in the sand at the beach or in a snowbank at

Growing Together

the park (be sure to use a duplicate box if you bury it in a public place—you don't want to risk losing your family's treasures!). You could hide it in your backyard or basement, in a neighbor's yard, or take it to a friend's or relative's house.

Finally, design a way for the kids to find the treasure. If it is buried in the sand or snow, you could give everyone a small shovel and "turn them loose" to dig until they find it. Or, you can prepare a map for them to follow. Carefully worded clues can also be fun. Example: "You'll have to search over rivers and through woods to find this treasure!" (This will take them to Grandmother's house, where you might have another clue to send them somewhere else.)

Once the treasure has been found, sit down together to open it and talk about what is inside:

- ▶ What kinds of things do we put into a treasure box? (Things that have great value; they cost a lot of money, or they have great meaning to us.)
- ▶ Pull out each family item, one at a time, and ask the kids to say why they think you included it in your treasure box.
- ▶ Take out the family Bible and ask why it was included. (God's Word is a treasure of guidelines to help us make wise choices. Learning what it says, and following these guidelines, is one of the wisest things we can do!)
- ▶ Look at the list of guiding questions, reminding everyone of the value of thinking through all our options before choosing one to try.
- ▶ Ask kids to name other items they might have included in the family treasure box, and tell why.

Growing Together

End your time by enjoying wherever you ended up (the beach, the park, someone's home), with lots of time for games and food!

2. Add the Next Two Phrases to Your CHOOSE Poster. Add the phrases "Own God's Word" and "One Choice to Try" to the next two lines on your poster, and learn the motions for them:

Hold your hands in front of you as if you are holding a book.

Raise index finger into the air, making a #1 sign.

PEANUTS   **By Schulz**

93 ▶

CHAPTER

FIVE

S=See It Through

GETTING READY

I'll Get Right to It...
First Thing Tomorrow!

T he first four steps of CHOOSE are all about *thinking* about the wisest choice we can make. The next step, **S = See It Through**, brings us to the point of *acting* on our choices. Now we must struggle with the difference between *deciding what to do* and *doing what we decided.* This is the stuff New Year's resolutions are made of. But of course, we don't have to wait until the New Year to make—and break—resolutions. I know. I'm really good at it, particularly in the area of diet and exercise programs. I have a million of them, all neatly filed away under *N*, for "Nice Try."

Learning to "see it through" in the area of diet and exercise has been a painful process for me. In the beginning, I would try to find the "perfect" plan by researching diet and exercise programs of all kinds and finally settling on the most comprehensive, healthiest program I could possibly set for myself. Then, with a great deal of optimism and excitement, I would make a firm commitment to start it right away—first thing in the morning. But somehow I didn't feel so optimistic or excited when the alarm went off at 5:30 A.M.! Invariably, within two days—a week, tops —my "perfect" plan was abandoned, and I was left, not with a wonderfully healthy body, but with intense feelings of failure.

Fortunately, the feelings of failure did not keep me from trying again. And with each new try I learned valuable lessons about seeing things through. All in all, I learned that there are three important skills needed to "see it through" successfully:

1. **Reality Checking.** Before trying to act on a choice, we need to run a reality check to be sure this choice is really the wisest *for us*. Sometimes the choice that looked the wisest on paper is not compatible with who we are or is so grandiose it simply is not achievable.

   When I first started choosing exercise programs, I was stuck in thinking that, since I am a "morning" person, the best time for me to exercise was early in the morning. What I was overlooking was how much I cherish starting my day by sitting quietly with my coffee cup in hand, engaging in reflection, prayer, and creative thinking. I finally realized that an early-morning exercise program that ignored my commitment to that time was doomed to failure, no matter how good it looked on paper. To "see it through" successfully, I needed to try some other options.

2. **Risk Taking.** Making choices that are truly wise will often move us outside of our comfort zones. The option we choose as the wisest may also be one that is very hard for us to do. For example, asking someone to forgive us, telling our loved ones what we need, or sharing our feelings with others are all wise choices. But they might also feel uncomfortable, especially if we never learned those particular communication skills. In those situations, "seeing it through" involves taking risks that may feel fearful or uncomfortable. This is the point at which we most often fail to "see it through." Our tendency is always to stay with what is easier and familiar, even if it is unhealthy.

   The point to remember is that taking a risk involves trying

out behaviors that are new to us. It is "risky" because we don't know whether or not we will be successful. Unfortunately, many of us have been so shamed by past failures that we are unwilling to risk anything that could potentially lead to failure and therefore more shame. The reality, however, is that there is no shame in taking a risk and failing. In fact, there can be no growth without taking—and learning from—risks. A wise friend once told me that, if I wasn't failing at some things on a regular basis, I wasn't risking (or growing) enough! Not unlike learning to ride a bicycle, we cannot learn healthier living skills if we are not willing to risk falling a few times along the way!

3. **Asking for Help.** In many cases, what we need most to "see it through" is help. Remember, it is not only okay to ask for help when we need it, it is one of the healthiest things we can do. In my quest for the perfect exercise program, I discovered that my follow-through increased significantly when I asked for help. Whether it was someone to whom I was accountable each week or someone who would diet or exercise with me, I needed to ask others to help. In the beginning, asking for help felt awkward and shaming; I'd rather start a diet and not tell anyone so I wouldn't be embarrassed two weeks later if I hadn't lost any weight. But as I grew in my ability to risk asking for help, I made an interesting discovery. When I spoke up and asked for help, I found many people in my life who were struggling with the same things and wanted help, too. So, together we were able to accomplish what none of us was able to do on our own.

It's not always easy to act on what we know to be the wisest choices for our lives. But we can do it! Making sure our choices are achievable, taking risks to face things outside our comfort zones, and asking for help when we need it are the keys to unlock the door of **S = See It Through!**

P.S. In spite of what I learned about follow-through, maintaining a consistent diet and exercise program is still a struggle. Some things in life are just like that!

F o r   R e f l e c t i o n

1. Make an assessment of your ability to "see it through" by ranking each item below on a scale of 1-10, one meaning that the statement is totally true of you:

   _____ I never follow through with the choices I make, especially if it means taking significant risks.

   _____ I am often paralyzed by fear of failure. I would rather not try than risk making a mistake and being shamed for it.

   _____ I never tell anyone when I make a major decision. That way I won't be embarrassed or shamed if I don't "see it through."

   _____ Overall, my comfort level with my ability to take risks and "see it through" is #_____.

2. List below any areas in which you have particular trouble with follow-through; i.e., diet and exercise, maintaining boundaries for your kids, managing compulsive behavior, etc.

   _____

   _____

   _____

3. In the areas you identified above, which of the three skills cause you the greatest problems:

—— Reality checking; I can't seem to make choices that are consistent with who I am and are achievable.

—— Risk taking; I most often stay with what is familiar and easy rather than risk failure or rejection.

—— Asking for help; I always keep my problems to myself.

—— Other insights: _____

_____

_____

4. Identify one decision you have made recently that seems to be difficult for you to "see through." Use the questions below to identify specific ways you can "see it through":

▶ Reality testing: Is it realistic for you and achievable?

_____

_____

_____

▶ Risk taking: Is there anything that feels frightening or difficult? Is there anything you simply don't know how to do?

_____

_____

_____

▶ Asking for help: Is there someone who could help you do this? Is there someone to whom you could be accountable for getting it done? _____

_____

_____

Building On
God's Word

Did you know that "seeing it through" was difficult for Jesus? Read Mark 14:32–42 and reflect on it in light of the discussion of this chapter. Write out your initial thoughts about Jesus' struggle with "seeing it through": _____

_____

_____

_____

Now read Hebrews 12:1–3 to discover how Jesus can be a significant help in our struggles to "see it through." In the space below, write a prayer asking Him to help you follow through in a specific situation in your life:

TALKING · TOGETHER

S =See It Through

Did you ever make a New Year's resolution? How long did you keep it? If you kept it longer than a week, you did very well! Many people make resolutions and don't keep them more than one day!

Making—and breaking—New Year's resolutions is an example of what **S = See It Through** is all about. The first four steps of CHOOSE helped us to *think* about the wisest choice we can make. In this next step, we learn

101 ▶

that it's not enough to think about what to do. We have to "see it through" and actually do it! It's here we discover that *deciding what to do* (steps 1–4) and *doing what we decided* (step 5) are two very different things.

It's not always easy to follow through and do what we decided. Here are three guidelines that can help:

1. **Make Sure Your Choice Is Realistic.**
    Sometimes the choice that seemed the wisest when we were thinking about it turns out not to be very wise for *us*. For instance, let's say you are having trouble with hitting your little brother when he does something that makes you angry. You may have decided that the wisest thing to do is never get angry with him again. Although that may be a *wise* choice, it is not a *realistic* one. No doubt your little brother will do something irritating again soon, and you *will* feel angry with him. A more realistic choice would be to find a better way to express your anger, like going to your room and hitting your pillow instead of hitting him.

2. **Talk About the Things That Feel Hard for You to Do.** Remember, the wisest thing to do is not necessarily the easiest! In fact, sometimes it is *easier* to do things that are *unwise*. For instance, it is easier to keep on hitting your brother when you are angry than to remember to go to your room and hit your pillow instead. Or, it is easier to lie than admit you did something wrong.

If we are going to "see it through" successfully, we have to learn to do things that are wise but feel hard or scary to do. We call that taking risks. The hardest thing about risks is that we don't know how they will turn out. Sometimes we make mistakes, or it takes a long time to learn how to do something new, like going to your room when you feel angry. Talking about the things that are hard helps us deal with them and learn new ways to handle them.

You don't need to be afraid of taking risks. In fact, you can only learn new things and grow by taking risks! Think about learning to ride a bicycle. You can't learn to ride until you're willing to fall down, get up, and keep trying. But once you learn how to do it, you can ride anywhere you want to go without thinking about what you're doing! So if you're taking a risk to learn something new, like not hitting your little brother, don't give up! It's okay if you make mistakes or forget sometimes. The point is to keep talking about it and working at it until you accomplish your goal!

3. **Ask for Help When You Need It.**
Sometimes the thing we need most to "see it through" is someone to help us. Even adults need to ask for help when they need it. Always remember—it's not only okay to ask for help when you need it, it's the wisest thing to do!

Each of the kids listed below has a good reason to ask for help. Unscramble the words to find out what those reasons are:

Suzanne feels _ _ _ _ _ _ _ _ .
N C S E O F D U

Morris feels _ _ _ _ _ _ _ _ _ _ .
T R H E D F I E G N

Jared feels _ _ _ _ _ .
N O L A E

Marsha just needs to
_ _ _ _ _ _ _ _ _ _ _ .
A T L K   O B U A T   T I

105 ▶

The Resolution

Denise walked into the house hoping no one was home. She didn't feel like talking to anyone just now, especially her brothers! Stopping inside the front door, she listened for sounds of life in the house. She was in luck—nobody was home.

Without even realizing what she was doing, she put her books on the table and went immediately to the kitchen and grabbed the cookie jar. She was in luck again—it was full. Oreos, too. How lucky can you get! She took a fistful and started twisting them open so she could scrape the creamy middle off with her teeth before crunching into the chocolate wafers.

Somewhere in the distance she heard a car door slam and the faint sound of someone calling her name. At the moment, however, chocolate wafers and creamy middles were all she cared about.

"Denise...Denise, where are you?" her mom yelled out as she stumbled through the back door, her arms overstuffed with groceries. "Oh, you're right here! Why didn't you answer me? I need some help with these — " she stopped in midsentence when she saw the cookie jar clutched tightly in her daughter's arms. "Uh, I take it things didn't go very well today."

Denise looked up, surprised by her mother's words. "Why do you say that?"

"You're eating cookies as if your life depended on it, and I know you. Whenever you get upset, you eat. Anything you can find... cookies, cake, ice cream, fried chicken...."

"I do not!" Denise shouted as she threw the cookie jar on the table as if it had suddenly become a hot potato. "I was hungry, that's all! I work hard at school, you know! It went fine today."

"Did it really?" Mom brightened and sat down next to her daughter. "Are you going to get a part in the school play?"

Denise looked away from her mom, grabbed

the cookie jar, and started eating again. "Yeah, well, maybe...I don't know yet," she said with her mouth full of cookies. "They said they'd post a list next week." She stuffed a whole Oreo in her mouth without bothering to open it up to eat the creamy middle first.

"Denise, stop it!" her mom said, prying the cookie jar out of her daughter's hands. "You promised you wouldn't do this anymore!"

"Do what?"

"Eat to cover up your feelings. We've talked this through a million times. Whenever you feel hurt, you eat instead of admitting you're hurting. No one   likes to feel hurt, honey, but it's okay!"

"That's easy for you to say!" Denise snapped back at her mom. "Besides, what's the big deal if I want an afterschool snack?" She reached for the cookie jar again.

"This isn't an afterschool snack, and you know it!" Mom responded, wishing she hadn't put that new package of Oreos in the cookie jar this morning. "What happened to the list of things you could do instead of eating when you feel hurt? What happened to your resolution to try some of those things the next time something hurtful happened?"

"It was a dumb resolution, that's what! It's too hard, Mom. I can't do it!"

Her mom sighed and stared down at the table for a moment. Then she looked up and said, "Yes, you can! And I can help. Will you let me help, Denise?"

There was a long pause while Denise struggled to find the courage to try something new. Then she smiled weakly at her mom and said quietly, "Okay...I guess."

"Great! Now, as I recall, the first thing on your list was to tell someone what happened and how you are really feeling. Do you want to talk about it?"

Denise brightened a little. "I really do want to tell you about the tryouts, Mom. They were so bad! But can we go to my room and talk? The boys will be home any minute and I don't want them to tease me."

"Sounds good to me!" Mom got up and once again took the cookie jar out of Denise's hands. "But let's leave these here, okay?"

"Okay," Denise said as she started for her room. Then she reached back into the cookie jar and wrapped her fingers around one Oreo. "But maybe I'll take just one more...just in case this talking stuff doesn't work!"

What do you think?

▶ Why did Denise eat cookies when she was feeling hurt? Why was this an unwise choice?

▶ Besides talking to someone about her feelings, what other choices do you think could have been on her list of things to do when she felt hurt?

▶ Is there something that feels as hard for you to do as giving up eating to cover her feelings was for Denise?

Remember...

Sometimes the wisest thing to do is not the easiest, but...

**You can "see it through"
by taking risks and asking for help
when you need it!**

Even Jesus knew that. Dying on the cross was hard for Him to "see through." But because He did it, He can help us when we have a hard time. Here's a verse from the Bible to remember:

Think about Jesus. He held on patiently while sinful men were doing evil things against him. Look at Jesus' example so that you will not get tired and stop trying. *Hebrews 12:3*

Growing Together

BUILDING ON GOD'S WORD

Memorize Hebrews 12:3. Make a memory puzzle by cutting 3 x 5 cards in half and printing one word of the verse on each card, including the reference. Mix the cards up and then work together to put them in the right order. Increase the fun by making two or more sets and having races to see who can do it the quickest.

Family Prayer Circle. Hebrews 12:3 tells us that Jesus understands how hard it is sometimes to "see it through." Stand in a circle and hold hands while you offer prayers asking Jesus to help you with the things that are hardest for you to "see through."

CONVERSATION STARTERS

Family Resolutions. Give each family member an opportunity to identify one area in which he or she is having trouble with follow-through. Examples might be remembering to brush teeth without being told; getting homework assignments finished on time; keeping diet-and-exercise programs; etc. Talk about what seems to be the biggest difficulty in "seeing it through." Then use these guidelines to help each family member find ways to improve follow-through:

1. **Reality testing:** Is it realistic for *you* and achievable?
2. **Risk taking:** Is there anything that feels frightening or difficult? Is there anything you simply don't know how to do?

Growing Together

3. **Asking for help:** Is there someone who could help you do this? Is there someone to whom you could be accountable for getting it done?

End your conversation time with a realistic resolution for each member of the family. Make a commitment to help one another follow through by giving lots of encouragement to each other and celebrating even tiny steps toward "seeing it through."

FAMILY NIGHT ACTIVITIES

1. **Plan a Family Project and "See It Through."** You can practice good follow-through skills in your family life by working together to plan and carry out a family project. Begin by preparing a list of possible projects. These might include things you have talked about doing but never accomplished. Take this as an opportunity to make a commitment to follow through on one of them. Possibilities:

Growing Together

▶ **Goal: Spending more time together as a family**

Possible Projects:

Plan a family outing or vacation

Complete a work project around the house

Calendar family meals and days together for the next year

Others: _____

_____

▶ **Goal: Building relationships with others**

Possible Projects:

Host a neighborhood block party

Visit elderly friends/relatives in nursing homes

Have a pizza party for new friends

Others: _____

_____

Growing Together

▶ **Goal: Reaching out to others in need**
Possible Projects:
Help serve meals at a local rescue mission or shelter for the homeless
Buy and deliver food to a local food shelf
Clean out closets of old clothes and toys and donate them to a local service agency
Offer to do cleaning and yard work for elderly neighbors
Others: _____

_____

Get the whole family involved in generating your list of possible goals and projects. Then let everyone share in choosing a project you can plan and do *together*. Here are a few guidelines to help you with the planning process:

❏ Apply the skills of follow-through you learned in this chapter: Do a reality check, identify the risks involved, and ask for help if you need it.

❏ Make a checklist of all the tasks that must be done to make this event happen. This includes things like sending out invitations, shopping, cleaning the house, contacting agencies, and so on.

❏ Decide when you will do each of the things on the checklist and *write these dates on your calendar*. Make a commitment that nothing will interfere with these times.

❏ Follow your checklist to accomplish your goal, and don't forget to celebrate a job well done when it's over!

Growing Together

2.   Add a Phrase to Your CHOOSE Poster. Add the phrase, "See It Through" to the next line on your poster, and learn the motions for it:

Make a ring around your eyes as if looking through binoculars.

CHAPTER

SIX

E=Evaluate
The Results

GETTING READY

Graceful Moments

*I*t was the morning after I had done my first ever fund-raising event. I was sitting at my desk "evaluating the results" when the phone rang.

"Hi, Linda," came the voice of a friend who knew how much I was struggling with learning how to do fund-raising. "How are you this morning?"

"Fine. I was just sitting here thinking about last night."

"That's why I called. I thought you'd be having a shame attack right about now."

"A what?" I was startled by his words.

"A shame attack. That was a pretty big risk you took last night."

"Okay, I confess. I don't have any idea what you mean by 'shame attack.' "

It was his turn to be startled. "You don't? Well, whenever I do something as risky and public as you did last night, I spend the next few days going over and over it in my mind, wondering what people thought of me, thinking about all the things I did wrong and how it could have been better—you know, stuff like that."

"Oh, well, I'm doing lots of that! In fact I'm making a list right now of all the mistakes I made and everything I want to do different next time. And I will admit I felt awkward and uncomfortable...but I don't see any *shame* in that. It's just par for the course when you're learning something new. Overall, I'm glad it went as well as it did."

"That's great! Most of the people I know have to struggle through lots of layers of shame to get to where you are right now. Must be terrific to be free from all that!"

I thought about that conversation for a long time afterward. Having taught CHOOSE in many settings, I knew that the step of "evaluating the results" has a powerful way of hooking shame in people and that many more people than I ever imagined have a deep-seated fear of being wrong. There seems to be something within the human experience that makes us want to deal with mistakes by covering up and hiding them.

So why wasn't I feeling shame? There were certainly lots of other places in my life where I struggled with great amounts of shame; why not now? I wondered if there was something in my life that gave me the freedom to evaluate the results of my choices, look honestly at the mistakes and imperfections, and not feel shamed by them. As I've thought about that in the time since, two characteristics have emerged as common to the people I know who effectively evaluate the results of their choices and grow from them:

1. ***Grace* Is an Important Part of Their Everyday Lives.** Although my home was not without its share of dysfunctions, I have a very vivid memory of my parents, and particularly my dad, that has always been a source of strength for me. On many occasions throughout my growing-up years, my dad would say, "Always remember, there is nothing you could ever do to change the fact that you are our daughter. No matter what happens, this will always be your home and you will

always have a place here." I even remember pushing him one day by saying, "But Daddy, what if I pulled out a gun and killed someone. What then?" He was quiet for a moment and then said, "Well, I guess we'd have to visit our daughter in jail!"

I didn't know it at the time, but the gift my father was giving me was permission to make mistakes—even big ones— with the full assurance that neither he nor my mom would "go away." Daddy didn't know much about God or the Bible, so he didn't know that what he was doing was modeling for me the truth of Romans 8:38, 39:

> Yes, I am sure that nothing can separate us from the love God has for us. Not death, not life, not angels, not ruling spirits, nothing now, nothing in the future, no powers, nothing above us, nothing below us, or anything else in the whole world will ever be able to separate us from the love of God that is in Christ Jesus our Lord.

This is what the Bible calls grace, and it is at the heart of our relationship with God—not our perfection but His acceptance of us in our imperfection. Grace is God's way of giving us room to grow. It is His assurance that no matter what happens, He will not go away or reject us as His sons and daughters. Grace is the antidote to the poison of shame. Receiving it gives us the power to see our mistakes as opportunities to grow rather than occasions for condemnation and shame.

No one likes to make mistakes, but making them is part of being human. When we evaluate the results and find we "blew it," we have a new choice to make. We can let shame guide us to hide our mistakes, or we can experience a graceful, or grace-filled, moment and move on.

2. **They *Celebrate* Small Steps.** Celebration is a powerful life experience that is too often restricted to the big events of our lives. One of the most effective methods of raising self-worth in ourselves and our children is to celebrate our growth. The step of **E = Evaluate the Results** gives us an occasion to affirm our successes in making wise choices, even when they are small—or perhaps *especially* when they are small! If you are in recovery, you have probably already figured out that one of the things our recovery groups do for us is give us a place to celebrate small steps of growth with people who understand how hard they were to achieve.

If you managed to stay sober one day, or you succeeded in expressing your anger in a healthier way, or you practiced a new listening skill and it worked—call someone and tell him or her about it, or write about it in your journal, or find another way to celebrate that fits you. Likewise, if you see little steps of growth in your children, be sure to affirm them with a compliment, a hug, or a note.

The importance of this last step cannot be overstated. To omit it is to rob you and your children of a whole host of opportunities for graceful moments and times of celebration.

F o r   R e f l e c t i o n

1. Describe below three experiences from your childhood that shaped your ability (or inability) to experience grace. _____

   _____

   _____

2. Describe below the last time you "evaluated the results" and *felt good* about embracing any mistakes or failures you found.

_____

_____

_____

_____

3. Describe below your most recent step of growth, no matter how small. _____

_____

_____

_____

_____

List at least three ways you could celebrate that step.

a. _____

b. _____

c. _____

Building On God's Word

Reread Jesus' story of the lost son, Luke 15:11–24, focusing particularly on the reaction of the father when his son comes home. Describe your feelings about that scene: _____

_____

_____

_____

Jesus told this story as an illustration of God's grace toward us. If you have trouble connecting with God's grace, try this simple prayer picture. Let yourself connect with your most hurtful mistake or failure. Then come to God in prayer, picturing yourself approaching Him from a long way off, as did the son in the story. Watch Him grow excited as He runs to meet you, and feel His arms close around you as you finally meet. Now tell Him of your failure and the shame you feel. When you have said all that is in your heart, read verses 22–24 and fill in your name wherever it says "him." Ask God to touch your heart and allow you to receive His grace and deep love for you in a way you have never received it before.

=Evaluate
The Results

E = Evaluate the Results means that, after all is said and done, we stop and think about the results of the choice we made. Was it a wise one? Are we happy with the way things turned out? Would we do the same thing again? Or was it an unwise choice and will we make a different one in a similar situation?

You may not know it, but you "evaluate the results" all the time. Have you ever heard yourself say:

- That movie was the best! I'm going to see it again as soon as I can!
- T-Ball is really fun! I'm going to try Little League when I'm old enough.
- Every time I play with Jonah I get in trouble. I don't think I want to play with him anymore.
- Star Crashers was too hard for me. I'm glad we rented it before I spent my birthday money to buy it.

Evaluating the results helps us do two things:

1. Celebrate the Wise Choices We Made. Making wise choices is hard work, and you deserve to celebrate when you make one. There's lots of ways to do that:

- You can go up on the roof and shout, "Hey, world! I made a wise choice and I'm happy about it!"
- You can tell someone in your family or call your best friend.
- You can hug somebody.

▶ You can write about it in your diary or journal.

▶ You can put a sign on your dog and parade him around the neighborhood.

▶ Your ideas:

_____

_____

It's especially important to celebrate when you chose to do something risky or new and it turned out well, even if it was a little thing. So, if you chose to do something like cleaning your room without being told or *not* getting mad when you lost a game or _____

_____

(fill in a wise choice you made recently)

Don't forget to celebrate!

2. Learn From Our Mistakes. Not every choice we make will be a wise one. Sometimes when we evaluate the results, we realize we made a mistake. Since making mistakes does not feel very comfortable, we may be tempted to blame someone else or throw a tantrum or withdraw and feel too ashamed to talk to anyone or try to hide it by lying about it. 127

Of course, no one likes to make mistakes. But the important thing to remember is that it is okay to say we made one. Everyone does once in a while, and when you are growing up it takes time to learn how to make wise choices. Sometimes the only way we really learn is by making a choice and then finding out that it wasn't such a great one after all.

So what do we do when we make a mistake? It's easy! We admit we made one and then take the time to think about what we could do different next time. And don't forget...if you need help, ask for it! Talking about our mistakes is the best way to learn from them!

Here's a way to practice. Look at each of the kids below and help them evaluate the results of the choices they made. First, decide what might happen next for each of them and write it on the line. Then check whether it was a wise or unwise choice:

1. I was sick all last week and didn't study my spelling words, so I cheated on the test today.

What will happen next: _____
☐ Wise Choice   ☐ Unwise Choice

2. My little sister tore my
favorite book. Instead
of yelling at her, I
went to my room and
hit my pillow.

What will happen next: _____
☐ Wise Choice   ☐ Unwise Choice

3. The boy who sits next
to me called me a jerk
at recess, so I punched
him in the nose.

What will happen next: _____
☐ Wise Choice   ☐ Unwise Choice

D Day

It was the worst day of the year so far. Report card day was never fun, but this one was absolutely, positively the worst day ever. Jocko didn't know how he would ever live through showing *this* report card to his dad. Two *D*s. His dad would be so disappointed!

He cringed as he saw Lana Fulbright rushing toward him from across the playground. "Hey, Jocko! How'd you do this time? All *C*s again, I bet! Well, mine is the same as always—all *A*s! By this time tomorrow, I'll be five dollars richer!" She waved her report card under Jocko's nose, fully enjoying humiliating him in front of all the other kids.

For reasons Jocko never understood, Lana fulfilled this little ritual every report card day. He suspected it had something to do with the frog he had put in her lunch box last year, but he wasn't sure. Usually he had some sort of way to get back at her, like telling her the only reason she got *As* was 'cause an alien from outer space secretly did all her homework, which he knew because he saw green slime on her papers—and in her hair! But today he didn't care what Lana thought about his report card—or the other kids, for that matter. His *dad*, however...well, that was another story.

Jocko dragged himself home, let himself in the front door of the empty house, and flopped on the couch. "Two more hours 'til dad gets home from work," he said to no one in

particular. "Maybe I can think up some excuses Dad would believe." His favorites were, "My teacher got me mixed up with somebody else when she made out the report cards," and, "Nobody needs this stuff when they grow up anyway," but they didn't seem good enough for *two D*s. What he needed was...Jocko tensed as he heard the key turn in the lock.

"Hey there, my man, how's it goin'?" his dad said as he threw his jacket on the chair and sat down next to his son. "Well, let's see it!"

This was it. Jocko handed the dreaded report card to his dad, feeling as if he were going to throw up. Dad was quiet for a long time, and then he sighed deeply. "Jocko, this is the worst one yet. What's this all about?"

"Would you believe my teacher got me mixed—"

"No. And don't even think of trying to come up with another one of your famous excuses. Let's cut right to the heart of the matter and talk about your Nintendo."

"I knew you were going to say that! That's not the reason, Dad, honest!"

"Jocko, I told you I was worried about your grades when your grandmother gave you that thing. You remember what you told me?"

"I said I'd only play when my homework was done."

"And did you?"

"Yes! Well, most of the time. Well...no, hardly ever."

"Looks to me as if you made some pretty unwise choices about how to use your Nintendo."

Jocko started to cry. "Dad, I'm really sorry! I'm just such a jerk. I'll never be smart like you, and I want to be so you'll be proud of me! Why can't I ever do anything right?"

"Whoa, wait a minute!" his dad responded, putting his arm around his son. "You didn't do anything to deserve all that! Just because you got two *D*s doesn't mean you're a jerk! It means you made some unwise choices, that's all. We'll just have to figure out how to make some other choices that will help you use the Nintendo in a way that won't interfere with your grades. I know you can do that, and this time I'll help. Now, let's go have dinner and then celebrate with a double-dip waffle cone at Bailey's."

Jocko brightened; Bailey's had the best waffle cones anywhere! "Okay...but, what do you mean *celebrate*? I just got the worst report card of my whole life and we're gonna celebrate? What are we celebratin'?"

Dad smiled. "Maybe just the fact that you are my son and I *am* proud of you! Let's go!"

What do you think?
- ▶ What unwise choices had Jocko made about using his Nintendo?
- ▶ How did Jocko expect his dad to react to the report card? How did his actual reaction help him accept his mistake and grow from it?
- ▶ Tell about a time you made an unwise choice and someone helped you admit it and grow from it.

Remember...

Taking time to evaluate the results will help you:

Celebrate your wise choices, and learn good things from your unwise ones!

Remember, too, that none of our unwise choices will ever stop God from loving and caring for us. Here's another important verse from the Bible:

Yes, I am sure that nothing can separate us from the love God has for us. Not death, not life, not angels, not ruling spirits, nothing now, nothing in the future, no powers, nothing above us, nothing below us, or anything else in the whole world will ever be able to separate us from the love of God that is in Christ Jesus our Lord.
Romans 8:38, 39

135 ▶

Growing Together

BUILDING ON GOD'S WORD

Play Bible Memory Verse Games. The three key verses presented in this book are important ones for all family members to know. Use a variety of memory verse games to learn Romans 8:38, 39 and review James 1:5 and Hebrews 12:3. Around the dinner table and just before bed are good times for working on verses. Adding a little friendly competition between family members can lend interest for older kids.

Memory Verse Games:

1. Memory Verse Circle, as detailed in chapter 1.
2. Memory Verse Race, as detailed in chapter 5.
3. Disappearing Words. Write a verse on a chalkboard and read it aloud together. Then choose a family member to erase two or three words. Now read it again, filling in the missing words. Continue letting family members erase words until you can say the whole verse from memory.
4. Balloon Pop. Print the verse references on small pieces of paper and place them inside balloons. Blow up the balloons and place them inside a large basket or trash bag. Make enough so every family member will get five balloons. For the next five days, let each family member choose a balloon, pop it, and say the verse that corresponds to the reference inside.

Growing Together

CONVERSATION STARTERS

CHOOSE Matching Game. Review the six steps of CHOOSE by playing a matching game. Write each of the steps on a separate 3 x 5 card and give them to family members. Then read each of the scenarios below, one at a time, and ask everyone who thinks he or she is holding the card with the corresponding step to lay the card faceup in the middle of the table. Have a discussion of why that card (or cards) was chosen, and come to a family agreement as to which step is correct.

1. Scott sees a new kid from his class standing on the playground by himself. Just as he starts to walk over to talk to him, his friends call: "Hey Scott! Let's go play ball!" Scott looks at the boy standing alone and then at his friends and asks himself, *What would Jesus do in this situation?*

2. Timothy had decided to tell his teacher he had cheated on the last spelling test. It was the hardest thing he ever had to do, but at recess today, he did it!

3. Jeremy got a *D* on his math test for the second time in a row. The first time he told himself he didn't care, but now he is determined to get a better grade next time!

4. After two days of not talking to her best friend, Jackie finally called her to say she was sorry. It felt so good to have her friend back again, she decided she would apologize even sooner the next time they had a fight!

5. After thinking a long time, Zelda finally decided to put her birthday money toward the new skateboard she has been saving up for instead of spending it at the toy store or going miniature golfing with her friends on Saturday.

6. Suzanne doesn't feel like cleaning her room. She thinks, *I could skip it and hope Mom doesn't notice; or I could ask Mom if I can wait until tomorrow; or I could just do it and get it over with!*

(see answers below)

FAMILY NIGHT ACTIVITIES

1. Wooden Spoon Puppet Role Plays. Using puppets is an effective way to get young children to apply the steps of CHOOSE to situations. Make it a family event by first making the puppets together. You will need:

About six wooden spoons in
    various sizes
Scraps of felt and yarn
Steel wool (optional)
Markers

First, draw the faces in the bowls of the spoons. Then use the felt, yarn, and steel wool (makes great hair) to develop them into characters. Make the larger spoons into adults that can be used as parents, grandparents, or teachers, and the

▶ 138

Answers: 1. O = Obey God's Word; 2. S = See It Through; 3. C = Claim the Problem; 4. E = Evaluate the Results; 5. O = One Choice to Try; 6. H = How Many Choices Can I Find?

Growing Together

smaller spoons into boys and girls. If you like, you can even make a simple puppet stage and backdrops for various kinds of scenes (indoors, outdoors, playground, etc.).

Using the scenarios listed in "Conversation Starters," make up little puppet plays to help the characters work through each step of CHOOSE. Once the kids get the idea, you can use the puppets to help them work through real situations in their lives.

2. Make CHOOSE Diaries. Older children can work through the steps of CHOOSE on paper. Involve them in making a diary they can use for this purpose. You will need:

Poster board for the covers
Copies of the CHOOSE worksheet
Stapler and markers

Make about ten copies of the CHOOSE worksheet (*see* page 141) for every family member and cut poster board to use as covers. Assemble the covers and work sheets into a booklet, and staple together. Use markers to decorate the covers.

Choose two or three of the scenarios listed in "Conversation Starters" as a way to practice using the diaries. Read each scenario and then use a diary page to work through each step of CHOOSE. When the kids can do it easily, have them use the diaries to work through real situations in their lives.

3. Add the Final Phrase to Your CHOOSE Poster and Have a Family Race. Add the final phrase, **E = Evaluate the Results**, to the last line of your poster and learn the motion for it.

Growing Together

Review all the steps on the poster with the hand motions and use them to have a family CHOOSE race. Divide into two teams (adults against kids works well), and race to see which team can say all the steps and do the hand motions the fastest!

Hold arms and hands as if in position of a pan scale and move them up and down as if weighing two things against each other.

Growing Together

I Always, Always Have Choices!

1. My problem: _____
_____
_____
_____

2. All my options:
   a. _____
   b. _____
   c. _____
   d. _____
   e. _____
   f. _____
   g. _____
   h. _____
   i. _____
   j. _____

3. The choice I will try is: _____
_____

4. Evaluating the results:
   ▶ Yes, it was a wise choice!
   ▶ No, it wasn't a wise choice. Next time, I'll try something different!

SUMMARY

*M*aking wise choices is an important skill for all of us to learn. Here are the key points to remember as you and your family grow in your ability to CHOOSE wisely:

▸ You always, always have choices — finding them will keep you from feeling powerless.

▸ The wisest choice is not always the easiest or most comfortable — taking risks is part of growing.

▸ Knowing what to do and doing it are two different things — be sure your choices are realistic and achievable!

▸ Asking for help when you need it is *always* a wise choice!

▸ It's okay to make mistakes — learning from them helps us grow.

And above all else . . .

. . . remember that God promises to help us choose wisely:

> If any of you needs wisdom, you should ask God for it. God is generous. He enjoys giving to all people, so God will give you wisdom. *James 1:5*